Family Circle | salad cookbook

Family Circle

SALAD
COOKBOOK

FAMILY CIRCLE LIBRARY OF CREATIVE COOKING
A Practical Guide to creative cooking containing special material from Family Circle Magazine and the Family Circle Illustrated Library of Cooking

ROCKVILLE HOUSE PUBLISHERS
GARDEN CITY, NEW YORK 11530

on the cover:
A help-yourself glass-filled delight of **Perfect Chef's Salad** will entrance both company and guests.

on the back cover:
Perk up a summertime table with **Cornucopia Salad** (top) or **Rio Rancho Supper Salad** and **Portuguese Seafood Salad** (bottom).

opposite the title page:
Create a help-yourself **Hero Salad** from this artfully displayed bowl of salad ingredients.

Publishing Staff
Editor: MALCOLM E. ROBINSON
Design and Layout: MARGOT L. WOLF
Production Editor: DONALD D. WOLF

For Family Circle
Editorial Director: ARTHUR M. HETTICH
Editor Family Circle Books: MARIE T. WALSH
Assistant Editor: CERI E. HADDA

Copyright © 1972, 1977, 1978 The Family Circle, Inc. All rights reserved under International and Pan-American Copyright Conventions.
Printed in the United States of America

A QUICK METRIC TABLE FOR COOKS

Liquid Measures

1 liter	4¼ cups (1 quart + ¼ cup or 34 fluid ounces)	1 gallon	3.785 liters
1 demiliter (½ liter)	2⅛ cups (1 pint + ⅛ cups or 17 fluid ounces)	1 quart	0.946 liter
1 deciliter (1/10 liter)	A scant ½ cup or 3.4 fluid ounces	1 pint	0.473 liter
1 centiliter (1/100 liter)	Approximately 2 teaspoons or .34 fluid ounce	1 cup	0.237 liter or 237 milliliters
1 milliliter (1/1000 liter)	Approximately 1/5 teaspoon or .034 fluid ounce	1 tbsp.	Approximately 1.5 centiliters or 15 milliliters

Weights

1 kilogram	2.205 pounds	1 pound	0.454 kilogram or 453.6 grams
500 grams	1.103 pounds or about 17.5 ounces	½ pound	0.226 kilogram or 226.8 grams
100 grams	3.5 ounces	¼ pound	0.113 kilogram or 113.4 grams
10 grams	.35 ounce	1 ounce	28.35 grams
1 gram	0.035 ounce		

Linear Measures

1 meter	1.09 yards or 3.28 feet or 39.37 inches	1 yard	0.914 meter
1 decimeter (1/10 meter)	3.93 inches	1 foot	0.3048 meter or 3.048 decimeters or 30.48 centimeters
1 centimeter (1/100 meter)	0.39 inch	1 inch	2.54 centimeters or 25.4 millimeters
1 millimeter (1/1000 meter)	0.039 inch		

Contents

	INTRODUCTION	6
1.	**MAIN-DISH SALADS**	6
2.	**MOLDED SALAD RICHES**	22
3.	**FRUIT SALAD SPECTACULARS**	48
4.	**RAINBOW OF SEAFOOD SALADS**	64
5.	**GARDEN FRESH SALADS**	74
	INDEX	95

Two main-dish salads to delight the family: **Rio Rancho Supper Salad** and **Portuguese Seafood Salad**.

Introduction

SALAD DAYS USED to mean green and fresh, and that still applies today. When the day is hot and the idea of working in the kitchen over a hot stove is too much, turn to the cool freshness of a salad.

So that you can find the type and the kind of salad you want—when you want it—this book is divided into special sections:

The first section presents many main-dish salads that will take you out of the kitchen and into the country or onto the patio. Also, there are some of the most popular dressings you drizzle over your favorite salads to enhance the flavor.

The prepare-ahead-and-cool-in-the-refrigerator salads are grouped next. A few minutes at the cutting and chopping board is usually enough. The rest is done by the refrigerator.

So that you can make a salad using ingredients on hand or because of a particular need, the next three sections are devoted to a dazzling array of fruit, seafood, and garden fresh vegetable salads.

Along the way, you'll discover salads that are as much fun to look at as they are to eat. So enjoy your **Salad Cookbook**.

Main-Dish Salads

Hot or cold, salads often work well as main-dish meals. Here they vary from international favorites to the main-dish salads grandmother made when you were young. And they vary from the elegant to the simple. So whatever type of main-dish salad suits your mood for the day, you'll find an example in these pages.

Rio-Rancho Supper Salad

Two varieties of canned beans plus crunchy fresh vegetables make this a hearty main dish

Makes 6 servings.

1 can (1 pound) chick peas, drained
1 can (1 pound) red kidney beans, drained
1 can (4½ ounces) pitted ripe olives, drained
1 cup sliced green onions
½ cup chopped parsley
1 to 2 cloves garlic, finely chopped
¾ cup Home-style Tomato Dressing (recipe follows)
1 package (8 ounces) Monterey Jack or Cheddar cheese, diced (2 cups)
1 cucumber, pared, seeded and diced
Chicory
¼ pound sliced salami or other cold cut
2 ripe tomatoes, cut into wedges
  OR: 1 pint cherry tomatoes

1 Combine chick peas, kidney beans, olives, green onions, parsley, garlic and dressing in large bowl; chill several hours.
2 Just before serving, stir in cheese and cucumber. Line salad bowl with chicory; mound bean mixture on top.
3 Fold salami slices and arrange around edge with tomatoes. Serve with crusty bread, if you wish.

Home-Style Tomato Dressing

This old favorite is sometimes made with tomato soup in place of the tomato sauce

Makes about 3 cups.

1 can (8 ounces) tomato sauce
½ cup red-wine or cider vinegar
1 small onion, cut up
2 tablespoons brown sugar
2 tablespoons Worcestershire sauce
1 teaspoon salt
1 teaspoon paprika
¼ teaspoon pepper
1 cup vegetable oil

1 Combine all ingredients except oil in container of electric blender; whirl until smooth.
2 Add oil gradually; continue blending until thickened and smooth.

Mediterranean Tuna Salad

Tuna prepared with Mediterranean accents makes a zesty and colorful salad

Makes 6 servings.

¼ cup tarragon vinegar
2 tablespoons lemon juice
1 clove garlic, minced
2 tablespoons chopped parsley
½ teaspoon leaf basil, crumbled
½ teaspoon salt
⅛ teaspoon pepper
½ cup olive oil
1½ pounds new red potatoes
1 cup sliced celery
2 cans (7 ounces each) tuna, drained and broken into chunks
1 jar (7 ounces) roasted red peppers
2 hard-cooked eggs, cut into wedges
1 can (2 ounces) flat anchovy filets
Lettuce
Lemon

1 Combine vinegar, lemon juice, garlic, parsley, basil, salt, pepper and oil in jar with tight-fitting lid; shake until well combined.
2 Wash potatoes well in cold water; cook in boiling salted water 20 minutes or until tender. Drain; cool, then slice. (Peel potatoes before slicing, if you wish.) Place potatoes and celery in a shallow bowl; pour dressing over; toss gently to coat potatoes well. Refrigerate and allow to marinate at least 2 hours. Refrigerate tuna, peppers, eggs and anchovies separately.
3 To serve, line a deep platter or shallow bowl with lettuce. Lift potatoes from dressing and

(continued)

8 • MAIN-DISH SALADS

arrange on top of lettuce; reserve dressing. Top with tuna, peppers and eggs. Arrange anchovies on top; drizzle with reserved dressing; garnish with lemon slices, if you wish.

Chicken and Avocado Salad

Canned chicken and chicken broth make this creamy Tex-Mex salad quick and easy

Makes 6 servings.

1 envelope unflavored gelatin
1 can (13¾ ounces) chicken broth
2 cans (5 ounces each) boned chicken or turkey
3 medium-size avocados
¼ cup lemon juice
¼ cup mayonnaise or salad dressing
1 teaspoon salt
¼ teaspoon cayenne
   TOMATO AND GREEN CHILI SAUCE (recipe follows)

1 Mix gelatin with ½ cup of the chicken broth in saucepan, let stand to soften 5 minutes; heat slowly over low heat, stirring constantly, just until dissolved.
2 Place chicken in large bowl; break up larger pieces of meat with a fork.
3 Halve avocados; remove pits; peel off skin. Cut avocado into large chunks; place in container of electric blender; add lemon juice, mayonnaise, salt and cayenne; cover. Whirl at high speed, adding a little chicken broth if necessary, just until mixture is smooth.
4 Turn blender to low speed; add remaining chicken broth and the gelatin mixture. Pour over chicken in bowl; mix well. Pour mixture into a 4- or 5-cup mold; chill several hours or until firm.
5 Loosen mold around edge with a thin-bladed knife; dip quickly in and out of a pan of hot water. Invert onto chilled serving plate; lift off mold. Spoon *Tomato and Green Chili Sauce* onto plate around mold, or serve separately. Serve with bowl of crisp mixed greens.

Tomato and Green Chili Sauce

Makes about 1¾ cups.

2 medium-size tomatoes, chopped (1½ cups)
½ cup chopped green onions
1 canned hot green chili pepper, chopped (2 tablespoons)
1 tablespoon red wine vinegar
1 tablespoon vegetable oil

Combine ingredients in a small bowl; toss to mix well. Chill 30 minutes or until serving time.

Ziti and Ham Salad With Mustard Dressing

This is a hearty salad for those who like it hot, hot

Makes 8 servings.

1 package (1 pound) ziti macaroni
1 tablespoon vegetable oil
1 canned (1 pound) ham
   OR: 1½ cans (12-ounce size) luncheon meat
1 can (about 4 ounces) sliced mushrooms, drained
2 cups diced green pepper
1 large red onion, diced (1 cup)
⅓ cup cider vinegar
1 tablespoon Worcestershire sauce
2 to 3 teaspoons dry mustard
1 teaspoon salt
8 drops liquid red-pepper seasoning
1 egg
⅔ cup peanut oil
2 tablespoons chopped fresh parsley
¼ cup grated Parmesan cheese
   Salad greens
1 can (14½ ounces) sliced tomatoes, chilled and drained

1 Cook ziti in boiling salted water, following label directions; drain; rinse; drain well. Place in bowl; toss with 1 tablespoon oil to prevent sticking.
2 Cut ham into strips about 2x¼-inches long; add with mushrooms, pepper and onion to ziti.
3 *To make Mustard Dressing:* Combine vinegar, Worcestershire, mustard, salt, red-pepper seasoning and egg in container of electric blender; cover; whirl at high speed for 15 seconds. Turn blender to low; add oil in a thin stream; continue blending 1 minute. Add parsley and cheese;

pour over ziti mixture in bowl. Toss to mix well; chill several hours.
4 *To serve:* Line a large salad bowl with crisp greens; spoon salad into bowl. Garnish with tomatoes.

Portuguese Seafood Salad

Shrimp and sardines are enhanced with flavors borrowed from the Iberian paella

Makes 6 servings.

- ½ package (1-pound size) orzo (1¼ cups)
- 1 can (4½ ounces) shrimp, drained
- 1 teaspoon finely chopped lemon rind (bright yellow part only)
- 4 tablespoons lemon juice
- 2 tablespoons finely chopped onion
- ¾ teaspoon salt
- 1 jar (6 ounces) marinated artichoke hearts
- ¼ teaspoon crumbled saffron threads
- 1 tablespoon warm water
- ½ cup cooked green peas
- 2 cans (about 4 ounces each) sardines
  Lettuce leaves
  Lemon slices
  Watercress

1 Cook orzo in boiling salted water, following label directions; drain; rinse with cold water; drain well.
2 Drain shrimp; rinse with cold water; place in large bowl; add lemon rind, lemon juice, onion, salt and artichokes with marinade. Soak saffron in warm water 5 minutes; add to bowl. Add the orzo and peas; toss well to mix. Refrigerate, stirring once or twice, at least 2 hours or until well chilled.
3 To serve, arrange the orzo mixture on lettuce leaves on a platter. Arrange sardines on top. Garnish with lemon and watercress.

Sauerkraut Salad With Corned Beef

An Old World favorite, sauerkraut takes on a new and delicious role in this make-your-own sandwich-salad

Makes 6 servings.

- 1 can (1 pound, 11 ounces) sauerkraut
- 1 medium-size onion, chopped (½ cup)
- ¼ cup chopped fresh dill
  or; 1 tablespoon dillweed
- 1 tablespoon chopped parsley
- ½ cup bottled Russian dressing
- 1 large green pepper, diced (about 1½ cups)
- 6 thin slices pumpernickel bread
  Mustard
  Romaine leaves or shredded lettuce
- 1 can (12 ounces) corned beef, chilled then sliced
- 1 package (8 ounces) sliced Swiss cheese
  Pickled red cherry peppers (optional)
  Fresh dill
- ½ cup sour cream
- ½ cup Russian dressing

1 Drain sauerkraut; rinse with cold water; drain well. Combine sauerkraut with onion, dill, parsley and dressing in a large bowl; toss to mix; chill until serving time.
2 Just before serving, add green pepper. Spread bread slices lightly with mustard. Line a shallow salad bowl with Romaine; arrange sauerkraut salad over half of lettuce; overlap slices of bread, corned beef and cheese on other half.
3 Garnish with cherry peppers and dill. Mix sour cream and Russian dressing and serve on side.

The Perfect Chef's Salad

You can vary this recipe by substituting ham or turkey for the chicken, and Swiss or Cheddar for the Bleu Cheese

Makes 6 servings.

- 2 whole chicken breasts
- 3 cups broken Boston lettuce
- 3 cups broken romaine
- 1 cup sliced celery
- 6 slices bacon
- 2 tomatoes, cut into thin wedges
- 1 ripe avocado
- 1 tablespoon lemon juice
- 3 hard-cooked eggs, sliced
- 4 ounces bleu cheese, crumbled
  Herb Vinaigrette Dressing (recipe follows)

1 Cook chicken; skin and bone; chill; then cut into thin slices.
2 Combine lettuce, romaine and celery in a large bowl; cover; refrigerate.
3 Cook and crumble bacon.

(continued)

4 Halve avocado; peel and pit. Cut into cubes; sprinkle with lemon juice.
5 Place tomatoes, avocado, chicken, bacon, eggs and cheese over greens.
6 Pour ⅓ of the HERB VINAIGRETTE DRESSING over the salad just before serving; toss gently to coat. Pass the rest of the dressing.

Herb Vinaigrette Dressing

Makes 1¼ cups.

¾ cup vegetable oil
½ cup tarragon-flavored vinegar
¾ teaspoon salt
¼ teaspoon seasoned pepper
¼ teaspoon leaf basil, crumbled

Shake all ingredients in a screw-top jar. Refrigerate to mellow flavors. Shake again just before pouring over salad.

Chef's Salad

This hearty meat-and-vegetable salad is always a favorite. Try it with warm buttered bread

Makes 6 servings.

1 chicken breast, weighing about 12 ounces
2 cups water
Few celery tops
1 small onion, halved
1½ teaspoons salt
¾ cup chili sauce
½ cup mayonnaise or salad dressing
1 teaspoon instant minced onion
½ teaspoon sugar
1 package (3½ ounces) sliced tongue, rolled in cone shapes
1 package (8 ounces) sliced cooked ham, cut in thin strips
8 ounces sliced Swiss cheese, cut in thin strips
1 large tomato, cut into wedges
1 small cucumber, pared and thinly sliced
1 hard-cooked egg, sieved
6 cups broken mixed salad greens

1 Combine chicken breast, water, celery, onion and 1 teaspoon of the salt in a medium-size saucepan; heat to boiling; cover. Simmer 30 minutes, or until chicken is tender. Remove from broth; cool. Chill about 45 minutes. Skin and bone, then cut chicken into bite-size cubes.
2 Blend chili sauce, mayonnaise or salad dressing, instant minced onion, sugar and remaining ½ teaspoon salt in a small bowl. Chill dressing for about 30 minutes.
3 Place greens in a large salad bowl. Arrange tongue, ham, chicken, Swiss cheese, tomatoes and cucumber slices in sections on top. Sprinkle the sieved egg over all.
4 Just before serving, spoon on dressing; toss.

Karrysalat

Curried herring and macaroni salad that hails from Norway

Makes 6 servings.

1 package (8 ounces) small macaroni shells
1 jar (12 ounces) herring party snacks in wine sauce
1 large Delicious apple, quartered, cored and diced (2 cups)
1 cup diced unpeeled cucumber
1 cup sliced red onion
¾ cup mayonnaise or salad dressing
¾ cup dairy sour cream
1½ teaspoons curry powder
Iceberg lettuce

1 Cook macaroni following label directions; drain.
2 Drain wine sauce from herring. Pour over hot macaroni shells in a large bowl; toss to coat.
3 Cut large herring pieces in half; add to bowl with apple, cucumber and onion.
4 Combine mayonnaise, sour cream and curry powder in a small bowl. Add to bowl; mix gently; cover. Refrigerate for several hours until the flavors are blended.
5 Just before serving line a salad bowl with lettuce; spoon salad on top.

Green Goddess Salad

The original version of this salad was created for George Arliss, star of "The Green Goddess," a stage play of 1915

Makes 6 servings.

⅓ cup light cream
1 cup mayonnaise or salad dressing

MAIN-DISH SALADS • 11

1 can (2 ounces) flat anchovies, drained
⅓ cup chopped green onions
⅓ cup chopped parsley
2 tablespoons chopped chives
1 package (1 pound) frozen cooked shelled and deveined shrimp
2 ripe avocados
2 tablespoons lemon juice
6 cups broken romaine
1 can (7 ounces) tuna fish, drained

1 To make dressing: Place cream, mayonnaise or salad dressing, anchovies, green onions, parsley and chives in container of electric blender; cover. Whirl until smooth, scraping down sides of blender container if necessary. Refrigerate at least 1 hour to blend flavors.
2 Cook shrimp following label directions; refrigerate.
3 Halve avocados; peel and pit. Cut into thin slices; dip in lemon juice.
4 Line a large shallow plate with romaine. Arrange shrimp and avocado slices on top. Place tuna in chunks in center. Garnish platter with lemon wedges. Pass Green Goddess dressing.

Greek Country Salad

This crispy vegetable and Feta cheese salad, a favorite throughout Greece, is catching on here in America

Makes 6 servings.

1 large head Iceberg lettuce
2 cups cherry tomatoes, sliced
1 large cucumber, sliced
1 cup sliced radishes
1 package (8 ounces) Feta cheese, cubed
2 cans (4 ounces each) skinless, boneless sardines, drained
½ cup pitted ripe olives, halved
½ cup chopped green onions
¼ cup chopped parsley
⅓ cup olive or vegetable oil
3 tablespoons lemon juice
½ teaspoon leaf oregano, crumbled
½ teaspoon salt
⅛ teaspoon freshly ground pepper

1 Line a large shallow bowl with lettuce leaves; break remainder into bite-size pieces into bowl.
2 Arrange tomatoes, cucumber, radishes, cheese, sardines, olives and green onions over lettuce. Sprinkle with parsley.
3 Combine oil, lemon juice, oregano, salt and pepper in a screw-top jar; shake well to mix.
4 Just before serving, shake salad dressing and drizzle over salad; toss lightly to mix.

Roquefort Mousse With Ham, Pineapple and Asparagus

Make this unusual creamy cheese mousse for a special occasion and your guests will be sure to rave

Makes 6 servings.

1 envelope unflavored gelatin
¼ cup lemon juice
¾ cup boiling water
4 ounces Roquefort cheese
2 medium-size cucumbers
1 tablespoon grated onion
½ cup finely chopped watercress
1 teaspoon salt
¼ teaspoon pepper
1 cup heavy cream
1 package (10 ounces) frozen asparagus spears
1 can (1 pound, 4 ounces) sliced pineapple in juice, drained
1 pound sliced, cooked ham
Boston lettuce

1 Sprinkle gelatin over lemon juice in a large bowl; let stand 5 minutes to soften. Add boiling water, stirring until dissolved; cool.
2 Pare cucumbers; cut in half lengthwise; remove seeds and shred coarsely. Drain thoroughly in a strainer.
3 Mash Roquefort with a fork in a medium-size bowl. Add cucumber, onion, watercress, salt and pepper. Stir until well-mixed. Add gelatin mixture.
4 Place bowl in a pan of ice and water; chill until mixture is syrupy-thick.
5 Beat heavy cream in a small bowl until stiff. Fold into Roquefort mixture. Spoon into a 4-cup mold; cover. Refrigerate about 4 hours or until firm.
6 Cook asparagus spears following label directions; drain and refrigerate.
7 Drain pineapple; cut slices in half.
8 Line a large platter with lettuce; unmold Roquefort mousse onto center of platter. Wrap ham slices around pineapple. Arrange ham, pineapple and asparagus around mousse.

MAIN-DISH SALADS

SALAD KNOW-HOW

Start with chilled, crackly-crisp greens. Use more than one variety—dark with light, mild with tangy—and tear, rather than cut, into bite-size pieces.

Choose your dressing carefully. A thin French dressing goes well with plain or mixed greens; a thicker French dressing or mayonnaise or salad dressing, with fruit, fish, vegetable or meat salads.

Keep the dressing simple, varying it with seasoning touches your family likes best. And be miserly, too, adding just enough dressing to coat the salad.

Use a light touch in tossing, reaching into the bottom of the bowl each time. Serve at once.

Bavarian Baked Potato Salad

This warm robust salad is chock-full of chunky frankfurters and cheese

Makes 6 servings.

- 5 medium-size potatoes (about 2 pounds)
- 1 pound frankfurters, cut into 1-inch pieces
- 2 tablespoons vegetable oil
- 1 medium-size onion, chopped (½ cup)
- 2 tablespoons all-purpose flour
- 3 tablespoons brown sugar
- 1 teaspoon salt
- 1 teaspoon dry mustard
- ⅛ teaspoon pepper
- 1 cup water
- ⅓ cup vinegar
- 1 cup thinly sliced celery
- ½ cup chopped green pepper
- ¼ cup chopped pimiento
- 8 ounces Cheddar cheese, sliced

1 Cook potatoes in boiling salted water in a large saucepan 30 minutes, or until tender; drain. Cool until easy to handle, then peel and dice. Place in a medium-size bowl.
2 Brown frankfurters in oil in a skillet; remove with a slotted spoon to the bowl with potatoes.
3 Sauté onion in same skillet until soft. Combine flour, sugar, salt and dry mustard; stir into drippings; cook, stirring constantly, until bubbly. Stir in water and vinegar; continue cooking and stirring until dressing thickens and bubbles 1 minute.
4 Add celery, green pepper and pimiento; cook 1 minute longer. Pour over potatoes and frankfurters. Spoon one half of the potato mixture into an 8-cup baking dish; layer with 4 slices of cheese; spoon remaining potato mixture into dish. Top with remaining cheese slices cut into triangles.
5 Bake in moderate oven (350°) 15 minutes, or until cheese is slightly melted. Serve salad warm.

Main-Dish Potato Salad a la Peloponnese

This money-stretching Greek recipe has cheese enough to boost it into the main-dish category. Greeks make it with feta, a crumbly, creamy-white, refreshingly salty goat cheese; use the feta cheese or, if you like, substitute with cottage cheese

Makes 6 servings.

- 2 pounds new potatoes, boiled until fork-tender, peeled and sliced fairly thin
- 2 tablespoons minced parsley
- 1 stalk celery, minced
- 1 small onion, peeled and minced
- ½ cup diced black or green (preferably Greek) olives
- 1 tablespoon grated Parmesan cheese
- ¼ teaspoon dillweed
- Pinch leaf rosemary, crumbled
- 1 teaspoon salt
- ¼ teaspoon freshly ground black pepper
- Juice of 1 lemon
- 2 tablespoons olive oil
- ¼ cup mayonnaise or salad dressing
- 8 ounces cream-style cottage cheese
- ⅓ to ½ cup milk (enough for good consistency)
- 6 tomato cups (optional)

1 Mix together potatoes, 1 tablespoon of the minced parsley and all remaining ingredients except tomato cups; cover and let "mellow" in refrigerator 2 hours or more.
2 Toss salad again, well; mound onto plates or, if you like, in tomato cups and sprinkle with the remaining tablespoon minced parsley.

Shrimps-Louis Dinner Salad

The summeriest of salads, with chunks of shrimps in a creamy dressing

Makes 6 servings

- ½ pound raw shrimps
- OR: 1 can (about 5 ounces) deveined cooked shrimps

¼ cup mayonnaise or salad dressing
¼ cup dairy sour cream
2 tablespoons chili sauce
1 teaspoon lime juice
½ teaspoon sugar
½ teaspoon grated onion
¼ teaspoon seasoned salt
1 large head of iceberg lettuce, broken into bite-size pieces (about 9 cups)

1 Shell and remove sand vein from fresh shrimps; simmer gently in water just to cover in small saucepan 3 to 5 minutes, or just until shrimps are pink. Drain; cool, then dice. (If using canned shrimps, rinse under running cold water before cutting up.)
2 Combine shrimps with remaining ingredients, except lettuce, in medium-size bowl; cover; chill at least 30 minutes before serving.
3 Fill a large salad bowl with lettuce; pour shrimp dressing over; toss to coat greens well.

Supper Salad

Main dish salad with a meat and cheese flavor

Makes 6 servings

2 packages (10 ounces each) frozen lima beans
1 medium-size onion, chopped (½ cup)
2 stalks celery, sliced
6 slices bacon, cut in pieces
¼ cup bacon drippings
¼ cup wine vinegar or cider vinegar
¼ teaspoon pepper
½ pound salami, cut into thin strips
1 package (8 ounces) sliced Swiss or American cheese, cut into thin strips
½ cup halved pitted ripe olives
3 medium-size carrots, pared and coarsely grated
3 slices sweet onion, separated into rings
   Few leaves of romaine
½ teaspoon salt
   Dash of paprika
   Vegetable oil and cider vinegar

1 Cook frozen lima beans, following label directions; drain. Place in salad bowl; add onion and celery.
2 Sauté bacon until crisp in medium-size frying pan; drain on paper toweling. Measure ¼ cup drippings; mix with ¼ cup vinegar and pepper; pour over lima beans in bowl; add bacon; toss lightly.
3 Arrange salami, cheese, olives and carrots in separate piles on top; place onion rings in middle; edge salad bowl with romaine.
4 Sprinkle salt and paprika over. Toss lightly, adding a little oil and vinegar, if needed.

Bouillabaisse Salad

Three seafood treats—scallops, salmon and haddock—go with vegetables and greens in a tomato-rich dressing.

Makes 6 servings

1 pound fresh sea scallops
   OR: 2 packages (7 ounces each) frozen sea scallops
1 slice onion
1 slice lemon
1 teaspoon salt
1 package (1 pound) frozen haddock fillets
   PIQUANT TOMATO DRESSING (recipe follows)
2 packages (9 ounces each) frozen artichoke hearts
2 packages (9 ounces each) frozen Italian green beans
6 cups broken salad greens
1 can (about 8 ounces) salmon, drained, boned and cut in chunks
6 small ripe tomatoes, peeled and cut in wedges
1 lemon, cut in 6 wedges

1 Wash fresh scallops in cold water; drain. (No need to thaw frozen ones.)
2 Fill a large frying pan with a 1-inch depth of water; season with onion, lemon and salt; heat to boiling. Add scallops; cover; remove from heat. Let stand 5 minutes for fresh scallops and 10 minutes for frozen ones; lift out with a slotted spoon and place in a large shallow dish.
3 Heat same pan of water to boiling again; add frozen haddock; cover. Simmer 5 minutes; remove from heat; let stand 5 minutes. Lift out with a wide spatula and place in dish with scallops. Drizzle each with ¼ cup of the PIQUANT TOMATO DRESSING; cover; chill.
4 Cook frozen artichoke hearts and Italian green beans in separate saucepans, following label directions; drain. Place in mounds in a large shallow dish. Drizzle each with ¼ cup of the PIQUANT TOMATO DRESSING; cover; chill.
5 When ready to serve, place 1 cup of the greens in each of 6 soup plates or shallow salad bowls. Cut haddock into ½-inch cubes; place

(continued)

Three main-dish salads to suit the heartiest of appetites: **Bouillabaisse Salad, Garden Vegetable Bounty,** and **Summer Potato "Chowder."**

with scallops, artichoke hearts, and green beans in separate mounds in each plate; pile salmon in centers. Tuck tomato wedges between fish and vegetables. Sprinkle scallops with chopped parsley, and haddock with paprika, if you wish. Serve with lemon wedges and remaining PIQUANT TOMATO DRESSING.

PIQUANT TOMATO DRESSING—Combine 1 cup olive oil or vegetable oil; ½ cup wine vinegar or cider vinegar; ½ cup tomato juice; 1 clove garlic, crushed; 2 teaspoons salt; 2 teaspoons sugar; and 1 teaspoon crushed fennel seeds in a jar with a tight-fitting lid; shake well to mix. Makes 2 cups.

Garden Vegetable Bounty

How invitingly colorful it looks with rings of seasoned vegetables, spinach, shredded red cabbage and bologna strips

Makes 6 servings

- 1 bag (1½ pounds) frozen mixed vegetables
- ⅔ cup bottled thin French dressing
- 1 package (10 ounces) fresh spinach
- 1 small head red cabbage (about 1½ pounds)
- 1 cup chopped celery
- ½ pound piece bologna, cut in thin strips
- ⅓ cup mayonnaise or salad dressing
- 4 teaspoons prepared mustard

1 Cook frozen vegetables in boiling salted water, following label directions; drain. Combine with ⅓ cup of the French dressing in a medium-size bowl; toss lightly to mix. Chill at least an hour to season and blend flavors. (Set remaining dressing aside for Step 5.)
2 Remove stems and any coarse ribs from spinach; wash leaves; dry well. Shred red cabbage fine.
3 Arrange spinach around edges in 6 soup plates or shallow salad bowls; place red cabbage in a ring around the spinach.
4 Stir celery into mixed vegetables; spoon into centers. Arrange bologna strips around vegetables.
5 Beat remaining ⅓ cup French dressing into mayonnaise or salad dressing and mustard in a small bowl. Serve separately with salads.

Summer Potato "Chowder"

Creamy bouillon dressing seasons vegetables while still warm for this salad twist on an old-timer.

Makes 6 servings

- 6 large potatoes
- 1 cup chopped green onions
- 2 cans (1 pound each) sliced carrots
- 2 envelopes instant chicken broth

MAIN-DISH SALADS • 15

1 teaspoon salt
1 teaspoon leaf basil, crumbled
¼ cup vegetable oil
¼ cup cider vinegar
¼ cup light cream or table cream
6 cups broken chicory or curly endive
2 packages (6 ounces each) sliced spiced ham
6 slices process American cheese (from an 8-ounce package)

1 Cook potatoes in boiling salted water in a large saucepan 30 minutes, or just until tender; drain; cool until easy to handle, then peel and slice thin. Layer with about three quarters of the green onions into a shallow dish.
2 Heat carrots to boiling in a medium-size saucepan; drain. Layer with remaining onions into a second shallow dish.
3 Combine chicken broth, salt, basil, vegetable oil, vinegar and cream in a jar with a tight-fitting lid; shake well to mix. Pour about ¾ over potato mixture and remaining over carrots. Chill at least 2 hours to season and blend flavors.
4 Divide chicory among 6 soup plates or shallow salad bowls; layer potato and carrot mixtures on top.
5 Stack each two slices of spiced ham with a slice of cheese between; cut in quarters, then cut each quarter in half diagonally to make triangles; arrange on top of salads. Garnish with parsley, if you wish

Rijsttafel Salad Platter

What a show-off! Everyone takes his choice of eight toppings to eat with tuna and salad-seasoned rice

Makes 6 servings

1½ cups uncooked regular rice
½ teaspoon curry powder
¼ cup bottled thin French dressing
½ cup mayonnaise or salad dressing
2 cans (7 ounces each) tuna, drained
1 can (8¼ ounces) pineapple chunks, drained
½ cup sliced green onions
½ cup roasted diced almonds (from a 5-ounce can)
1 cup sliced celery
3 hard-cooked eggs, shelled and chopped
½ cup chopped radishes
½ cup toasted flaked coconut (from an about-4-ounce package)
1 small avocado, peeled, halved, pitted and diced

1 Cook rice, following label directions; drain; place in a medium-size bowl. Stir curry powder into French dressing in a cup; drizzle over hot rice; toss lightly to mix. Chill at least an hour to season.
2 When ready to serve, stir in mayonnaise or salad dressing; spoon onto a large platter.
3 Separate tuna into chunks; mound on top of rice salad in center of platter; pile pineapple tidbits, onions, almonds, celery, eggs, radishes, coconut and avocado, spoke fashion, around edge. Garnish tuna with a radish rose, if you wish. Serve with more French dressing.

Chicken Salad Deluxe

Tender chicken is brightly flavored with a sour-cream–mayonnaise combination

Makes 4 servings

1 broiler-fryer (about 3 pounds)
4 cups water
1 small onion, sliced
  Few celery tops
¼ teaspoon salt
⅓ cup mayonnaise or salad dressing
⅓ cup dairy sour cream
1 tablespoon lemon juice
¼ teaspoon pepper
¾ cup chopped celery
1 medium-size onion, chopped (½ cup)
¼ cup chopped dill pickle
  Lettuce
  Paprika

1 Combine chicken with water, sliced onion, celery tops and salt in a kettle or Dutch oven. Heat to boiling; reduce heat; cover; simmer about 1 hour, or until chicken is tender. Remove from broth and cool until easy to handle. (Save broth to start a soup another day.)
2 Skin the chicken and take meat from bones. Cut meat into bite-size pieces; put in medium-size bowl.
3 Blend mayonnaise or salad dressing, sour cream, lemon juice and pepper in a small bowl. Combine celery, onion and dill pickle with chicken; add the dressing; toss until evenly coated. Cover; chill at least an hour to season and blend flavors.
4 Line salad bowl with lettuce leaves. Spoon salad into bowl. Sprinkle with paprika.

16 • MAIN-DISH SALADS

Cornucopia Salad Bowl

It takes time to put this salad together, but the stunning result is worth all the effort

Makes 6 servings

- 2 cans (16 ounces each) hominy, drained
- 1 can (12 or 16 ounces) whole-kernel corn, drained
- 1 cup diced celery
- ½ cup sliced green onions
- 6 tablespoons bottled thin French dressing
- ½ teaspoon salt
- ¼ teaspoon pepper
- 1 package (9 ounces) frozen Italian green beans
- 1 head of Boston lettuce
- ½ cup prepared sandwich spread
- 1 package (8 ounces) sliced salami

1 Combine hominy, corn, celery, green onions, 4 tablespoons of the French dressing, salt and pepper in a large bowl; chill at least an hour to season and blend flavors.

2 Cook green beans, following label directions; drain. Combine in a small bowl with remaining 2 tablespoons French dressing; chill along with hominy mixture.

3 When ready to serve, line a large shallow bowl with lettuce; shred any remaining and place in bottom of bowl. Stir sandwich spread into hominy mixture; mound on top of shredded lettuce.

4 Fold salami slices into cornucopia shapes, or cut into strips or small pieces; arrange in a circle on top. Pile seasoned green beans in center. Garnish with a twist of pimiento, if you wish.

Barbecued Chicken Supper Salad

Ready-cooked meat and salad come from your supermarket; you add the creative touch.

Makes 4 servings

- 2 containers (1 pound each) prepared macaroni salad

Don't settle for just any summertime salad. Let **Cornucopia Salad Bowl** grace your dining table.

MAIN-DISH SALADS • 17

1 package (4 ounces) shredded Cheddar cheese
1 can (8 ounces) lima beans, drained
½ cup chopped celery
½ teaspoon fines herbes
1 small head chicory, washed, dried, and separated into leaves
2 medium-size tomatoes, cut in wedges
2 ready-to-eat barbecued chickens, weighing about 2 pounds each
Sweet mixed pickles
Stuffed green olives

1 Combine macaroni salad, cheese, lima beans, celery, and herbes in a large bowl; toss lightly to mix well. Chill at least an hour to season.
2 Just before serving, line a large platter with chicory leaves; break remaining into bite-size pieces in center; spoon macaroni salad on top. Tuck tomato wedges around salad.
3 Cut chickens in half with kitchen scissors; place, skin side up, around edge of platter.
4 Thread pickles and olives, alternately, onto wooden picks; stick, kebab style, into macaroni salad. Serve with rye-bread-and-butter sandwiches, if you wish.

Lazy-Susan Chef's Salad

Set out big bowls so everyone can toss his own to suit his taste

Makes 8 servings

1 package (12 ounces) assorted sliced cold cuts
1 package (8 ounces) sliced Swiss cheese
1 package (8 ounces) sliced caraway cheese
1 package (8 ounces) sliced process American cheese
1 large red onion, peeled, sliced, and separated into rings
1 bunch radishes, washed and trimmed
1 large cucumber, halved and sliced thin
1 package (about 4 ounces) garlic-flavor croutons
2 small heads romaine, washed and dried
GARLIC DRESSING (recipe follows)

1 Slice cold cuts and cheeses into thin strips. Arrange with onion, radishes, cucumber, and croutons in separate dishes on a Lazy Susan, or pile in separate mounds on a large serving platter.
2 Break romaine into bite-size pieces; place in another bowl in the center.
3 Serve with GARLIC DRESSING.

GARLIC DRESSING—Combine 1 cup olive oil or vegetable oil, ½ cup wine vinegar or cider vinegar, 1 clove garlic, minced, and a dash each of salt and pepper in a small jar with a tight-fitting cover; shake well to mix. Shake again before serving. Makes 1½ cups.

Antipasto Platter

Your refrigerator dividend: An inviting meal of cold sliced meat and cheese, plus four salad-style vegetables

Makes 6 servings

2 medium-size yellow squashes, trimmed and cut in 2-inch-long sticks
1 package (10 ounces) frozen asparagus spears
1 package (9 ounces) frozen artichoke hearts
¾ cup bottled Italian salad dressing
SALAD TOMATOES (recipe follows)
1 head Boston lettuce, washed and separated into leaves
6 slices cold cooked beef
1 package (8 ounces) sliced Edam cheese
1 small cucumber, scored and sliced thin

1 Cook squashes in boiling salted water in a medium-size saucepan 10 minutes, or just until tender; drain. Cook asparagus spears and artichoke hearts in separate medium-size saucepans, following label directions; drain.
2 Place vegetables in separate piles in a large shallow dish; drizzle with Italian dressing. Chill at least an hour to season.
3 Prepare SALAD TOMATOES; chill.
4 Just before serving, line a large tray with lettuce; arrange beef and cheese slices, alternately, in a row on top. Arrange squashes, asparagus, artichoke hearts, tomatoes, and cucumber slices in separate piles around edge. Serve with Italian bread and prepared mustard, if you wish.

SALAD TOMATOES—Wash 1 pint cherry tomatoes and stem; place in a small bowl. Combine 2 tablespoons chopped parsley, ½ teaspoon seasoned salt, ½ teaspoon sugar, dash of pepper, 2 tablespoons olive oil or vegetable oils, 1 tablespoon cider vinegar, and 1 teaspoon prepared mustard in a jar with a tight-fitting lid; shake well to mix. Pour over tomatoes. Chill at least an hour to season. Makes 6 servings.

MAIN-DISH SALADS

Picnic Chef's Salad

It travels beautifully with all the makings packed separately

Makes 8 servings

- 1 head of leaf or Boston lettuce
- 1 head of romaine
- 1 bunch of watercress
- 1 bunch of green onions
- 1 bunch of radishes
- ½ pound sliced corned beef, cut in thin strips
- ½ pound sliced process American cheese, cut in thin strips
- ½ pound sliced process Swiss cheese, cut in thin strips
- 4 hard-cooked eggs, shelled and quartered
- 1 cucumber, sliced
- 1 bottle (10 ounces) stuffed green olives, drained
- 1 package (about 4 ounces) croutons
  Vegetable oil
  Cider vinegar
  Salt and pepper

1 Wash and drain salad greens well; wash and trim onions and radishes. Wrap separately in transparent wrap or foil, or pack in plastic bags; chill until picnic time.
2 Line 2 baskets or deep trays with transparent wrap; arrange greens and onions in one; place meat, cheeses, eggs, cucumber, radishes and olives in separate mounds in another; cover both lightly to keep foods moist. Leave croutons right in their own package.
3 At serving time, set out all the makings with salad bowls for each to make his own salad.

Chicken Salad Mimosa

This salad is so bold that guests will want seconds

Makes 4 to 6 servings

- 4 chicken breasts, weighing about 12 ounces each
- 1¾ teaspoons salt
  Few celery tops
- 2 cups water
- 1 cup chopped celery
- 2 tablespoons chopped green onions
- 2 tablespoons chopped pimiento
- 1 bottle (8 ounces) coleslaw dressing
- 3 tablespoons lemon juice
- ⅛ teaspoon pepper
  Romaine
- 2 tablespoons toasted slivered almonds
- 1 hard-cooked egg, shelled and cut up

1 Combine chicken breasts with ¼ teaspoon of the salt, celery tops and water in a large frying pan. Heat to boiling; cover. Simmer 30 minutes, or until chicken is tender. Remove from broth; cool until easy to handle, then pull off skin and take meat from bones; dice meat. Combine with celery, green onions and pimiento in a medium-size bowl.
2 Blend coleslaw dressing, lemon juice, remaining 1½ teaspoons salt and pepper in a small bowl. Pour over chicken mixture; toss lightly to mix. Chill at least 2 hours to season.
3 When ready to serve, line a large salad bowl with romaine. Add almonds to chicken mixture; toss lightly; spoon into bowl. Press hard-cooked egg through a sieve over top.

Double Salad Jumbo

Luscious for luncheon: seasoned asparagus and carrots and crunchy chicken salad, perched on golden waffles

Makes 6 servings

- 2 cups diced cooked chicken
- 1½ cups diced celery
- 1 tablespoon chopped parsley
- ½ teaspoon seasoned salt
- ¼ cup mayonnaise or salad dressing
- 1 can (1 pound) sliced carrots, drained
- 1 can (about 15 ounces) asparagus spears, drained
- 3 tablespoons bottled thin French dressing
- 12 frozen waffles
  Boston lettuce
  Pretzel sticks

1 Combine chicken with celery, parsley and seasoned salt in a medium-size bowl; fold in mayonnaise or salad dressing. Chill at least 30 minutes to season and blend flavors.
2 Place carrots and asparagus in separate piles in a shallow dish; drizzle French dressing over all. Chill at least 30 minutes to season.
3 Just before serving, toast waffles, following label directions; place 2 on each of 6 serving plates; top each with several leaves of lettuce.

4 Spoon ½ cup chicken salad on one waffle on each plate; arrange carrots and asparagus in bundles on remaining waffles. Garnish each plate generously with pretzel sticks.

POPULAR SALAD DRESSINGS

Green Goddess Dressing

This great classic is from California

Makes 2½ cups.

1 teaspoon leaf tarragon, crumbled
¼ cup tarragon vinegar
1 cup mayonnaise or salad dressing
1 carton (8 ounces) dairy sour cream
½ cup chopped fresh parsley
2 tablespoons chopped chives
2 tablespoons anchovy paste
1 tablespoon lemon juice
1 clove garlic, minced

1 Soak tarragon in vinegar 10 minutes; strain vinegar into small mixing bowl; discard tarragon.
2 Blend mayonnaise or salad dressing, sour cream, parsley, chives, anchovy paste, lemon juice and garlic into vinegar; cover; chill 1 to 2 hours. Use to dress crisp green salads.

Mock Hollandaise

A fast, foolproof version of the French classic plus two delectable variations

Makes 1¼ cups.

¾ cup mayonnaise or salad dressing
½ cup milk
1 tablespoon lemon juice
½ teaspoon salt
⅛ teaspoon pepper

Combine the mayonnaise or salad dressing, milk, lemon juice, salt and pepper in a small saucepan. Heat slowly, stirring constantly, just until hot. Serve hot, over cooked asparagus.

Variations
CURRY À LA CRÈME—Combine ¾ cup mayonnaise or salad dressing, ½ cup milk and 1 teaspoon of curry powder in a small saucepan. Heat slowly, stirring constantly, just until hot. Serve sauce hot, over cooked whole onions. Makes about 1¼ cups.
SAVORY MUSTARD—Combine ¾ cup mayonnaise or salad dressing, ¼ cup milk and 2 tablespoons prepared horseradish-mustard in a small saucepan. Heat slowly, stirring constantly, until hot. Serve hot, over cooked carrots. Makes about 1 cup.

Mayonnaise

Have the experience of making it from scratch at least once

Makes 1¾ cups.

2 egg yolks
1 teaspoon dry mustard
½ teaspoon salt
Dash white pepper
4 tablespoons lemon juice
1½ cups vegetable oil

1 Beat egg yolks until thick and lemon colored in a deep bowl, with an electric mixer set at high speed. Beat in dry mustard, salt, pepper and 2 tablespoons of the lemon juice.
2 Lower speed of mixer to medium and *drop by drop* add oil to bowl until ½ cup of the oil has been added. Increase the speed of oil addition to a thin stream and beat in until another ½ cup of the oil has been added.
3 Beat in remaining 2 tablespoons lemon juice, then oil in a slow stream until mixture is thick and creamy.

NOTE—If you add oil too quickly and mixture begins to separate, beat 1 egg yolk in a second deep bowl; gradually beat in mayonnaise mixture, until smooth and well blended. For thinner mayonnaise, stir in a drop or two of hot water.

MAIN-DISH SALADS

Home-Style Salad Dressing

A touch of Parmesan cheese and a dash of Italian herbs give character to this dressing

Makes 1 cup.

- ⅔ cup vegetable oil
- ½ cup cider vinegar
- 2 tablespoons grated Parmesan cheese
- 1 teaspoon salt
- 1 teaspoon mixed Italian herbs, crumbled
- ¼ teaspoon pepper

Combine vegetable oil, vinegar, cheese, salt, mixed Italian herbs and pepper in a jar with a tight-fitting lid. Shake well. Chill to blend flavors.

Russian Dressing

To make this really Russian—and worth its weight in gold—stir in a tablespoon of black caviar

Makes 1½ cups.

- 1 cup mayonnaise or salad dressing
- ⅓ cup bottled French dressing
- 2 tablespoons catsup
- 2 tablespoons chopped green pepper
- 1 tablespoon minced onion
- ½ teaspoon prepared horseradish

Mix mayonnaise or salad dressing, French dressing, catsup, green pepper, onion and horseradish in a small bowl. Use to dress green salads.

Thousand Island Dressing

Rich and thick—not for calorie counters

Makes 1¾ cups.

- 1 hard-cooked egg, finely chopped
- 2 teaspoons minced onion
- 1 cup mayonnaise or salad dressing
- ¼ cup catsup or chili sauce
- 2 teaspoons sweet pickle relish
- 2 teaspoons minced pimiento-stuffed green olives
- Dash white pepper
- 4 tablespoons lemon juice
- 1½ cups vegetable oil

1 Beat egg yolks until thick and lemon colored in a deep bowl, with an electric mixer set at high speed. Beat in dry mustard, salt, pepper and 2 tablespoons of the lemon juice.
2 Lower speed of mixer to medium and *drop by drop* add oil to bowl until ½ cup of the oil has been added. Increase the speed of oil addition to a thin stream and beat in until another ½ cup of the oil has been added.
3 Beat in remaining 2 tablespoons lemon juice, then oil in a slow stream until mixture is thick and creamy.

NOTE If you add oil too quickly and mixture begins to separate, beat 1 egg yolk in a second deep bowl; gradually beat in mayonnaise mixture, until smooth and well blended. For thinner mayonnaise, stir in a drop or two of hot water.

Strawberry Pink Dressing for Fruit Salads

Try this on colorful combinations of cottage cheese and fresh fruit, or spoon it over a molded salad

Makes 1¼ cups.

- 1 cup whole strawberries
- ¾ cup cream-style cottage cheese
- 3 tablespoons lemon juice
- 2 tablespoons sugar

Combine all ingredients in container of electric blender and whip on high speed until smooth.

Cottage Cheese Snow

Fluffy with whipped cream and lightly spiced with ginger, it's a perfect complement to fresh fruits

Makes 6 servings.

- ½ cup heavy cream
- 2 tablespoons sugar
- ½ teaspoon ground ginger
- 1 pound cream-style cottage cheese
- ½ teaspoon grated lemon rind

Beat cream with sugar and ginger until stiff in a small bowl; fold into cottage cheese and lemon rind in a medium-size bowl. Chill until serving time.

POPULAR SALAD DRESSINGS • 21

Blue Cheese French Dressing

Try this on any green salad or pour over tomatoes

Makes 1¼ cups.

- ⅔ cup vegetable or olive oil
- ½ cup cider or wine vinegar
- ½ teaspoon sugar
- 1 teaspoon salt
- ¼ teaspoon pepper
- ⅓ cup coarsely crumbled blue cheese (about 1½ ounces)
- 1 clove garlic, peeled and minced

Combine all ingredients in a screw-top jar with a tight-fitting lid. Shake well to blend; chill.
VARIATION: PARMESAN DRESSING—Substitute ½ teaspoon leaf basil, crumbled; ½ teaspoon leaf tarragon, crumbled; and 2 tablespoons grated Parmesan for the blue cheese and garlic in recipe above. Makes 1 cup.

Creamy Blue Cheese Dressing

This is delicious with almost any tossed green salad or with a fresh shrimp and celery mixture

Makes about 1½ cups, or enough for 6 servings.

- ½ cup mayonnaise or salad dressing
- ½ cup dairy sour cream
- ½ cup crumbled blue cheese (2 ounces)
- 1 tablespoon lemon juice
- ¼ teaspoon salt
  Few drops liquid red-pepper seasoning

Blend all ingredients in a small bowl. Cover; chill. Pour over salad greens.

Classic French Dressing

This is one of the most popular salad dressings and it couldn't be easier to make

Combine ⅔ cup vegetable or olive oil, ½ cup cider vinegar or wine vinegar, 1 teaspoon of salt, ½ teaspoon sugar and ¼ teaspoon pepper in a jar with a tight-fitting lid. Shake well to blend; chill. Great for green salads. Makes 1 cup.

Variations

HERBED FRENCH DRESSING—Combine 1 cup CLASSIC FRENCH DRESSING with 2 tablespoons grated Parmesan cheese, ½ teaspoon crumbled leaf basil and ½ teaspoon crumbled leaf tarragon in jar with tight-fitting lid. Shake well to blend; chill. Refreshing for crispy vegetable salads. Makes 1 cup.
TOMATO FRENCH DRESSING—Combine 1 cup CLASSIC FRENCH DRESSING with 1 can condensed tomato soup, 1 tablespoon of prepared mustard, 1 tablespoon minced onion and 1 halved garlic clove in a large jar with tight-fitting lid. Shake well to blend and chill. Delightful on crisp, chilled lettuce wedges. Makes 2⅓ cups.
BLUE CHEESE FRENCH DRESSING—Combine 1 cup of the CLASSIC FRENCH DRESSING with ⅓ cup of coarsely crumbled blue cheese and 1 clove of minced garlic in a jar with a tight-fitting lid. Shake it well to blend the flavors; chill. Zesty on ripe red tomatoes.
TANGY FRESH DRESSING—Combine 1 cup CLASSIC FRENCH DRESSING with 1 teaspoon Worcestershire sauce, 1 teaspoon of prepared mustard and 1 halved garlic clove in a jar with a tight-fitting lid. Shake it well to blend; chill. Great for marinating cooked asparagus, green beans or sliced yellow squash. Makes 1 cup.

Dressings help spark up a salad. But, often, the simple oil and vinegar combination is all that is necessary.

Molded Salad Riches

Heap up the goodness and fold or cover with gelatin and you have a molded salad. Lend them all the goodness of a full meal and you have a main-dish molded salad. In these pages you'll chance upon many main-dish and side-dish molded salads.

Chicken Mousse in Aspic

Shimmering aspic sparkles around a smooth creamy chicken or turkey mousse—a perfect party make-ahead

Makes 6 servings.

- 2 cans condensed chicken broth
- 3 envelopes unflavored gelatin
- 2½ cups diced cooked chicken or turkey
- 1 can (3¾ ounces) liver pâté
- 1 tablespoon prepared mustard with horseradish
- 1 cup heavy cream, whipped
- 6 thin slices cooked ham
  Pimiento
  Celery tops
  Parsley

1 Empty broth into a 4-cup measure; add enough water to make 4 cups. Sprinkle gelatin over 1 cup of broth mixture in small saucepan; let soften 5 minutes. Heat slowly, stirring constantly, until gelatin is completely dissolved; add to remaining broth. Pour 1 cup into a 9x9x2-inch baking pan; chill until set (for decorating platter).
2 Whirl diced chicken or turkey with 1¾ cups of remaining gelatin mixture, ⅓ at a time, in container of electric blender until smooth. Turn into a large bowl; stir in liver pâté and mustard. Chill mixture until it is thick enough to mound softly when spooned; fold in whipped cream. (This is the mousse.)
3 Meanwhile, roll the thin ham slices into cone shapes; fit inside foil cones *(directions follow)*. Refrigerate. Pour about ⅓ cup gelatin into a 5-cup ring mold; set in a pan of ice and water (chill remaining gelatin until syrupy). When almost set or sticky-firm, arrange cutouts of pimiento and celery or parsley leaves on gelatin; spoon about ¼ cup of the chilled syrupy gelatin over and around decorations.
4 Spoon mousse into a pastry bag fitted with a large notched tip; pipe mousse into cones to fill them; place on a rack so they won't roll around; chill. Pipe a generous layer of mousse on top of the gelatin in mold, leaving a space next to side of mold. Spoon remaining gelatin down side of mold, then pipe in remaining mousse; smooth out top. Chill several hours, or until completely set.
5 To unmold: Loosen around edges with a small knife; dip mold quickly in and out of a pan of hot water. Cover with serving plate; turn upside down; shake gently to release mousse; lift off mold. Remove filled cones from foil molds. Arrange cones in center of mold with parsley.
6 Cut gelatin in square pan into cubes; spoon around mold. Keep refrigerated until ready to serve.

FOIL CONES

For each cone, tear off a 6-inch piece of heavy-duty foil from an 18-inch-wide roll. Fold each piece in thirds to make a square; fold crosswise to make a triangle. Using center of longest side of triangle as tip of cone, start at one side and roll up to form a cone.

Party Salmon Platter

Fancy molded salad is its company star to frame with zippy-seasoned vegetables

Makes 6 to 8 servings

GLAZED SALMON MOLD *(recipe follows)*
- 2 medium-size yellow squashes
- 1 package (10 ounces) frozen Fordhook lima beans
- 1 can (1 pound) sliced beets, drained
- 1 envelope onion salad-dressing mix
  Cider vinegar
  Vegetable oil
- 1 head Boston lettuce, separated into leaves

(continued)

An all-season favorite, **Chicken Mousse in Aspic** features chicken, ham, whipped cream, liver pate, and mustard for a combination that is sure to please.

MOLDED SALAD RICHES

1 Prepare GLAZED SALMON MOLD and chill.
2 Wash yellow squashes; trim ends, then quarter each lengthwise; cut in 2-inch sticks. Cook, covered, in a small amount of boiling salted water in a medium-size frying pan 20 minutes, or until crisply tender; drain.
3 Cook lima beans, following label directions; drain. Place squashes, beans, and beets in separate shallow dishes.
4 Prepare salad-dressing mix with vinegar, water, and salad oil, following label directions. Drizzle part over each vegetable; cover. Chill at least an hour to season and blend flavors.
5 When ready to arrange platter, place GLAZED SALMON MOLD in the center of a large platter. Arrange lettuce cups around edge; fill with seasoned vegetables. Garnish with sprigs of fresh dill, onion rings, pimiento strips and dill-pickle slices, if you wish.

Glazed Salmon Mold

A shimmering mold that will lend excitement to any table

Makes 6 to 8 servings

  1 can (1 pound) salmon
  1 can (about 7 ounces) crabmeat
  2 hard-cooked eggs, shelled and chopped
  1 cup finely diced celery
  ¾ cup mayonnaise or salad dressing
  1 tablespoon lemon juice
  1 teaspoon grated onion
  ¼ teaspoon freshly ground pepper
  1 envelope unflavored gelatin
  1 envelope instant vegetable broth
    OR: 1 vegetable bouillon cube
  2 cups water
    Few drops liquid red pepper seasoning
  10 radishes, sliced thin
  ¼ small green pepper, cut in thin strips
  1 slice stuffed olive

1 Drain salmon; flake finely, removing any dark bits of skin. Drain crabmeat; flake and remove bony tissue, if any. Combine both with chopped eggs and celery in a large bowl.
2 Blend in mayonnaise or salad dressing, lemon juice, onion and pepper. Spoon into a 6-cup fish-shape mold, packing down well with back of spoon; cover. Chill at least an hour.
3 While mold chills, soften gelatin with vegetable broth or bouillon cube in water in a small saucepan. Heat, stirring constantly and crushing cube, if using, with a spoon, just until gelatin dissolves; remove from heat. Stir in liquid red pepper seasoning; cool at room temperature. (For a slightly pink color, stir in 1 teaspoon beet liquid from can.)
4 Unmold salmon mold by running a sharp-tip thin-blade knife around top to loosen; invert into a jelly-roll pan; lift off mold.
5 Measure ⅔ cup of the cooled gelatin mixture into a small bowl; place in a larger bowl partly filled with ice and water. Chill, stirring several times, 2 to 3 minutes, or until as thick as unbeaten egg white. Spoon over salmon mold to make a layer. Chill until gelatin is firm.
6 Arrange sliced radishes on top of gelatin for fish "scales," pepper strips for "tail" and "fins," and olive slice for "eye."
7 Chill another ⅔ cup gelatin mixture, following Step 5; carefully spoon over decorations on top of mold. Chill again until firm. Chill remaining gelatin; spoon over top to make a thick coating, then chill mold at least 4 hours, or until very firm. (Overnight is even better.)
8 When ready to serve, trim away any excess gelatin around bottom of mold. Lift mold onto a large serving platter with two wide spatulas or pancake turners.

Stuffed Lobster

French-dressing marinade gives this lobster its tart spicy flavor

Makes 8 servings

  8 frozen South African lobster tails (3 or 4 packages, 10 ounces each)
  1 lemon, sliced
  1 tablespoon mixed whole spices
  ⅔ cup bottled thin French dressing

1 Cook lobster tails in boiling salted water with lemon and mixed whole spices, following label directions; drain.
2 When shells are cool enough to handle, cut with scissors through thick membrane on each side where it joins hard shell; remove membrane. Take out lobster meat by peeling hard shell back with one hand and pulling meat out with the other. Chill shells for Step 4.
3 Cut lobster meat into bite-size pieces; place in a large bowl; pour French dressing over, tossing lobster lightly until coated. Cover; chill several hours.
4 Spoon marinated lobster into shells, dividing evenly.

For a colorful table, set **Stuffed Lobster** around a **Shimmering Shrimp Aspic**.

Cucumber-Rice Ring with Stuffed Lobster

Pair this cucumber-topped rice salad with stuffed lobster for a party meal

Makes 8 servings

Cucumber Layer

- 1 envelope unflavored gelatin
- 2 tablespoons sugar
- 1 teaspoon salt
- 1½ cups boiling water
- ¼ cup lemon juice
- ½ cucumber, sliced thin

Rice-Salad Layer

- 8 cups cooked rice (2 cups uncooked)
- 2 cups chopped celery
- 6 hard-cooked eggs, chopped
- ½ cup chopped green pepper
- ½ cup chopped pimientos
- ½ cup chopped parsley
- ¼ cup chopped stuffed green olives
- 1 envelope unflavored gelatin
- 2 teaspoons salt
- ½ cup water
- ½ cup cream for whipping
- 2 cups mayonnaise or salad dressing
  STUFFED LOBSTER (recipe follows)
  Lettuce
  Lemon slices

(continued)

26 • MOLDED SALAD RICHES

1 Make cucumber layer: Mix gelatin, sugar and salt in 2-cup measure; stir in boiling water until gelatin is dissolved; stir in lemon juice. Chill until syrupy-thick.
2 Place a 12-cup mold in a larger bowl of ice and water; pour ½ cup syrupy gelatin into mold; arrange a ring of cucumber slices, overlapping, on top. Let layer set until sticky-firm, then carefully spoon remaining syrupy gelatin over; chill until sticky-firm.
3 Make rice-salad layer: Combine rice, celery, eggs, green pepper, pimientos, parsley and olives in large bowl.
4 Soften gelatin with salt in water in a 1-cup measure; heat over hot water until dissolved; cool.
5 Beat cream until stiff in medium-size bowl; fold in mayonnaise or salad dressing; stir in cooled gelatin mixture until well blended; fold into rice mixture. Spoon over sticky-firm cucumber layer in mold; chill 12 hours or overnight, or until firm.
6 To unmold, run a sharp-tip thin-blade knife around top of mold, then dip mold *very quickly* in and out of a pan of hot water. Or, after loosening around top, tip mold from side to side, shaking gently to loosen gelatin from side enough to break vacuum at bottom. Cover mold with serving platter; turn upside down, then gently lift off mold.
7 Arrange STUFFED LOBSTER on lettuce around mold; tuck in lemon slices.

Shimmering Shrimp Aspic

Any hostess will win raves with this aspic

Makes 6 servings

- 3 cans (13¾ ounces each) chicken broth
- 3 envelopes unflavored gelatin
- 2 packages (1 pound each) frozen deveined shelled shrimp
- Watercress
- Pitted ripe olives, slivered
- 1 cup mayonnaise or salad dressing
- 2 tablespoons lemon juice
- 1 teaspoon grated onion
- 3 hard-cooked eggs, shelled and coarsely chopped
- ½ cup diced celery

1 Skim fat from chicken broth.
2 Soften gelatin in chicken broth about 5 minutes in a large saucepan. Heat, stirring constantly, until gelatin dissolves. Pour into a medium-size bowl; cool.
3 Cook shrimp, following label directions; drain; cool. Set aside 6 shrimp for decoration; cut remainder into bite-size pieces; place in a large bowl; cover; chill.
4 Pour ½ cup of the cooled gelatin mixture into an 8x8x2 pan; chill. (Use for platter decoration in Step 10.)
5 Pour ½ cup of the remaining gelatin mixture into a 9x5x3 loaf pan. Chill until sticky-firm.
6 Arrange reserved whole shrimp, with watercress sprigs and olives on the aspic in loaf pan to make a pretty design. Spoon ½ cup of the remaining gelatin mixture carefully over the design, a little at a time, chilling briefly after each addition. Then chill completed design layer till it is sticky-firm.
7 Stir mayonnaise or salad dressing and lemon juice into remaining gelatin mixture. Place bowl in a pan of ice and water to speed setting. Chill, stirring several times, until as thick as unbeaten egg white.
8 Fold in onion, chopped eggs, shrimp and celery. Pour carefully over sticky-firm aspic layer in loaf pan. Chill until firm, about 4 hours. (Overnight is best.)
9 Just before serving, loosen salad around edges with a knife; dip pan *very quickly* in and out of hot water. Cover pan with serving plate; turn upside down; gently lift off pan.
10 Cut small triangles from firm aspic in square pan. Arrange as decorative border around salad. Chill until serving time.
11 To serve, cut salad into 6 slices; garnish each serving with some of the aspic triangles.

Patio Crab Salad with Louis-Dressing Mold

Delicately flavored crabmeat is complemented with fresh pineapple, dill and a tangy cheese-dressing mold

Makes 6 servings

- 3 packages (about 6 ounces each) frozen king crabmeat, thawed
- 2 tablespoons lemon juice
- 1 small ripe pineapple
- LOUIS-DRESSING MOLDS (recipe follows)
- Romaine
- Fresh dill
- 6 lemon wedges

1 Drain and pick over crabmeat, removing any bits of bone but keeping meat in big chunks; place in medium-size bowl; sprinkle evenly with lemon juice; cover; chill.

2 Cut 6 thin slices from pineapple; cut away skin and "eyes," then cut each slice into 3 fan-shape pieces; snip off core from tip of each fan.
3 Arrange 3 pineapple pieces in fan shape, a mound of crabmeat and a LOUIS-DRESSING MOLD on romaine in individual salad bowls; garnish with fronds of dill and a lemon wedge; serve with chopped dill to sprinkle over, if you like.

Louis-Dressing Molds

These individual molds accompany Crab Salad

Makes 6 molds

- 1 envelope unflavored gelatin
- ¼ cup cold water
- ½ cup hot water
- 2 teaspoons sugar
- 2 tablespoons lemon juice
- 1 cup mayonnaise or salad dressing
- ¼ cup chili sauce
- ½ cup cream for whipping
- ½ cup crumbled blue cheese

1 Soften gelatin in cold water in small bowl; add hot water and sugar; stir until dissolved; add lemon juice.
2 Beat in mayonnaise or salad dressing and chili sauce until creamy-smooth; stir in cream and blue cheese.
3 Pour into six 4-ounce molds or custard cups; chill until firm; unmold and serve with PATIO CRAB SALAD.

Chicken Indienne

The curry gives this chicken molded salad its Indian heritage

Makes 6 servings

- 2 envelopes unflavored gelatin
- 1 tablespoon sugar
- 1 teaspoon curry powder
- 3½ cups canned chicken broth
- 2 tablespoons lemon juice
- ⅓ cup chutney (from a 6-ounce bottle), finely chopped
- 4 cups diced cooked chicken
- 1 cup chopped celery

(continued)

Although it looks like a summery chicken and grape molded salad, **Chicken Indienne** is a curry, with the chutney sealed beneath a mound of grapes.

28 • MOLDED SALAD RICHES

1 Soften gelatin with sugar and curry powder in 1 cup of the broth in a medium-size saucepan; heat, stirring constantly, just until gelatin dissolves; remove from heat. Stir in remaining 2½ cups broth.
2 Measure ½ cup of the gelatin mixture into a small bowl; set aside for next step. Stir lemon juice into remaining gelatin in saucepan. Chill about 50 minutes or until as thick as unbeaten egg white.
3 Stir chutney into gelatin in small bowl; pour into a 6-cup mold; chill about 30 minutes or just until sticky-firm.
4 Fold chicken and celery into thickened gelatin in saucepan; spoon over sticky-firm chutney layer in mold. Chill several hours, or overnight, until firm.
5 To unmold, run a sharp-tip thin-blade knife around top of mold, then dip *very quickly* in and out of a pan of hot water. Cover mold with serving plate; turn upside down; gently lift off mold. Garnish with leaves of Belgian endive, halved seedless grapes and flaked coconut, if you wish.

Salmon Supper Mold

Freshly cooked salmon steak is the star of this fluffy main-dish salad

Makes 6 servings

1 fresh or frozen salmon steak (about ¾ pound)
4 peppercorns
1 teaspoon salt
1 slice of lemon
1 slice of onion
   Handful of celery leaves
   Water
1 envelope unflavored gelatin
1 envelope instant vegetable broth
1½ cups water
1 teaspoon grated onion
1 teaspoon lemon juice
⅛ teaspoon pepper
   OR: Few drops liquid red pepper seasoning
½ cup mayonnaise or salad dressing
1 cup chopped celery

1 Simmer salmon steak with peppercorns, ½ teaspoon salt, lemon and onion slices and celery leaves in just enough water to cover in a medium-size frying pan, 15 minutes, or until salmon flakes easily with a fork.
2 Lift out carefully with a slotted spatula; drain on paper toweling until cool enough to handle, then remove skin and bones. Flake salmon; place in a small bowl. (There should be about 1½ cups.) Set aside for Step 4.
3 Soften gelatin with vegetable broth in 1 cup of the water in a medium-size saucepan over medium heat, stirring constantly, just until gelatin dissolves. Stir in remaining ½ water, onion, lemon juice, remaining ½ teaspoon salt, pepper or red pepper seasoning. Chill 30 to 40 minutes, or until as thick as unbeaten egg white.
4 Stir in mayonnaise or salad dressing; fold in salmon and celery. Spoon into a 4-cup mold; chill several hours, or until firm.
5 Just before serving, run a sharp-tip thin-blade knife around top of mold, then dip mold *very quickly* in and out of a pan of hot water. Invert onto serving plate; carefully lift off mold. Serve with lemon wedges to squeeze over, or with your favorite bottled tartare sauce, if you wish.

Glazed Tuna-Salmon Mold

This gourmet specialty takes a bit of fussing, but it's really easy to make

Makes 6 to 8 servings

2 cans (about 7 ounces each) tuna, drained and finely flaked
2 cans (about 8 ounces each) salmon, drained and finely flaked
2 hard-cooked eggs, shelled and sieved
1 cup finely diced celery
1 can (about 5 ounces) water chestnuts drained
2 tablespoons chopped parsley
1 teaspoon grated onion
1 cup mayonnaise or salad dressing
1 tablespoon lemon juice
½ teaspoon prepared mustard
   Few drops liquid red pepper seasoning
2 envelopes unflavored gelatin
1 envelope instant chicken broth
1 teaspoon salt
2 cups water
½ small onion, sliced thin
2 cups ice and water
1 slice stuffed olive
1 pimiento, cut in thin strips

1 Combine tuna, salmon, sieved eggs and celery in a large bowl.

MOLDED SALAD RICHES • 29

2 Slice 8 water chestnuts very thin and set aside in a cup for making fish "scales" in Step 7. Chop remaining very fine and stir into salmon mixture with parsley and onion.
3 Blend mayonnaise or salad dressing, lemon juice, mustard and red pepper seasoning in a 2-cup measure; fold into salmon mixture. Spoon into a 6-cup fish-shape mold, packing down well with back of spoon; cover. Chill at least 2 hours.
4 While salmon chills, soften gelatin with chicken broth and salt in the 2 cups water in a small saucepan; add onion. Heat slowly, stirring constantly, until gelatin dissolves. Strain over ice and water in a 4-cup measure, stirring until ice melts.
5 Pour 2 cups gelatin mixture into a shallow pan, 9x9x2; chill 2 hours, or until firm, to use for garnish in Step 8. Let remaining gelatin stand at room temperature 15 minutes, or just until as thick as unbeaten egg white.
6 While gelatin stands, unmold fish this way: Run a sharp-tip thin-blade knife around top to loosen; invert onto large serving platter; lift off mold.
7 Spoon a thin layer of slightly thickened gelatin from Step 5 over molded fish to coat completely. (Some of the gelatin will run off into platter, making a base for garnish in Step 8.) Set olive slice in place for "eye," strips of pimiento for "mouth," "tail" and "fins" and sliced water chestnuts for "scales." Carefully spoon another layer of gelatin over top. Chill a few minutes, or until sticky-firm, then spoon on any remaining thickened gelatin to make a smooth coating. Chill until serving time.
8 Just before serving, cut gelatin in pan into small squares; spoon around mold on platter. Garnish with lemon wedges dipped in chopped parsley, if you wish.

Sun-Gold Potato Mold

This party-size classic, molded prettily in an angel-cake pan, looks so inviting with its bright egg topper

Makes 12 to 16 servings

15 medium-size potatoes
⅓ cup vegetable oil
3 tablespoons cider vinegar
1 tablespoon grated onion
2 teaspoons salt
1 teaspoon leaf basil, crumbled
1 teaspoon dry mustard
⅛ teaspoon pepper
6 hard-cooked eggs, shelled
1 cup chopped green pepper
1 cup chopped sweet red pepper
1 cup chopped celery
1 cup mayonnaise or salad dressing
¼ cup milk

1 Cook potatoes in boiling salted water in a large saucepan 45 minutes, or just until tender; drain. Peel while still warm; cut into small cubes; place in a very large bowl. (There should be about 12 cups.)
2 Combine vegetable oil, vinegar, onion, salt, basil, mustard and pepper in a 1-cup measure; pour over potatoes; toss lightly until dressing is absorbed.
3 Halve 2 eggs; remove yolks and set aside in a cup for Step 6. Chop egg whites and remaining 4 eggs; add to potatoes with green pepper, red pepper and celery.
4 Blend mayonnaise or salad dressing and milk in a small bowl; fold into potato mixture.
5 Spoon into a 10-inch tube pan; press down lightly with back of spoon to make top even; cover. Chill several hours to season and blend flavors.
6 When ready to serve, loosen salad around edge and tube of pan with a thin-blade knife; invert pan over serving plate; let salad slide out; lift off pan. Press saved egg yolks through a sieve onto top of salad. Garnish with tiny sprigs of parsley, if you wish.

Salmon in Aspic

This is an unusual salad for a special occasion

Makes 12 servings

1 whole fresh salmon, dressed (about 4 to 5 pounds)
1 tablespoon salt
1 bay leaf
1 large onion, sliced
½ cup lemon juice
  Water
  LEMON ASPIC (recipe follows)
3 hard-cooked eggs, shelled and sliced
6 pitted ripe olives, sliced
  Fresh dill fronds
3 medium-size tomatoes
1 cup mayonnaise or salad dressing
2 tablespoons chopped fresh dill
  Lemon wedges
  Chicory

(continued)

30 • MOLDED SALAD RICHES

When the buffet is special, let **Salmon in Aspic** steal the thunder

1 Wash salmon under running cold water; place flat on rack in a large shallow pan (use fish poacher or roasting pan). Add salt, bay leaf, onion, and lemon juice, then add water to half cover fish.
2 Heat to boiling; reduce heat; cover. Simmer 15 to 20 minutes, depending on thickness of fish. Remove pan from heat; let fish cool in stock for 1 hour.
3 Lift rack, holding until well drained; transfer to serving platter by sliding fish or by turning over onto platter. Remove skin carefully. Chill salmon while making LEMON ASPIC.
4 Spoon a small amount of chilled aspic over fish to coat evenly; chill until sticky-firm; repeat. Spoon any aspic that runs off back into bowl.
5 Arrange eggs, olives, and small fronds of dill on fish; spoon aspic over in thin layer; chill until sticky-firm. Repeat 2 or 3 more times until all aspic is used and fish and garnish are well-coated with aspic. (This can be done early in the day or even day before.) Chill until very firm.
6 Before serving, scoop out tomatoes with a spoon to make cups; dice enough of centers and tops to make ½ cup; drain cups and diced tomato well. Combine mayonnaise or salad dressing with diced tomato and dill; mound into tomatoes.
7 Arrange tomatoes, lemon wedges, chicory, and diced aspic on fish platter.
8 To serve, loosen top layer of fish from backbone; cut into pieces. When top half has been served, remove backbone in one piece and slice and serve the second half.

LEMON ASPIC—Soften 2 envelopes unflavored gelatin in ½ cup cold water in a small bowl; add ¼ cup sugar, 1 teaspoon salt, and 2½ cups boiling water; stir until gelatin is dissolved. Stir in ½ cup lemon juice and ¼ teaspoon liquid red pepper seasoning. Measure 1 cup aspic mixture into an 8x8x2-inch pan. Chill remainder until thick as unbeaten egg white; use this to coat fish; Chill aspic in pan until firm; dice for garnishing fish.

Raspberry Cream Mold

A shimmering delight topped with frozen whipped dessert

Makes 8 servings

1 package (6 ounces) raspberry-flavor gelatin
2 cups boiling water
¼ cup lemon juice
1 can (1 pound, 14 ounces) fruit cocktail
½ cup mayonnaise or salad dressing
1 container (4½ ounces) frozen whipped dessert topping, thawed
1 cup tiny marshmallows

1 Dissolve gelatin in boiling water in a large bowl; stir in lemon juice.
2 Drain syrup from fruit cocktail into a cup, then stir syrup into gelatin mixture; beat in mayonnaise or salad dressing.
3 Place bowl in a deep pan of ice and water to speed setting. Chill, stirring several times, until as thick as unbeaten egg white.
4 Stir in whipped topping; fold in marshmallows and fruit cocktail. Spoon into an 8-cup mold. Chill several hours, or overnight, until firm.

5 When ready to serve, unmold onto a serving plate. Frame salad with small lettuce leaves, if you wish.

Dilled Shrimp in Aspic

A flavorful shrimp salad imported from Denmark

Makes 6 servings

1 package (1 pound) frozen shelled deveined shrimp
1 medium-size cucumber
2 tablespoons chopped fresh dill
1 tablespoon minced onion
2 tablespoons lemon juice

½ teaspoon salt
⅛ teaspoon pepper
2 cans (13¾ ounces each) chicken broth
2 envelopes unflavored gelatin
2 tablespoons lemon juice
  Pimiento
  Dill fronds
  CREAMY DRESSING (recipe follows)

1 Cook shrimp, following package directions; drain; cool. Pick out several even-size shrimp; reserve for decoration. Cut remaining shrimp into ¼-inch pieces; place in a medium-size bowl.
2 Cut half the cucumber into very thin slices; reserve for decoration. Pare and seed remaining half of cucumber; cut into ½-inch pieces; place in bowl with diced shrimp. Stir in chopped dill, onion, 2 tablespoons of the lemon juice, salt,

(continued)

and pepper. Let stand 1 hour to season. Drain well.

3 Skim fat from chicken broth; discard. Soften gelatin in 1 cup of the broth about 5 minutes in a small saucepan. Heat, stirring constantly, until gelatin dissolves; stir into remaining chicken broth in a medium-size bowl. Add remaining 2 tablespoons lemon juice. Cut out decorative shapes from pimientos.

4 Pour ½ cup of the gelatin mixture into bottom of a 6-cup ring mold; place in a large bowl filled with mixture of ice and water until mixture is sticky-firm. Quickly arrange reserved shrimp, cucumber slices, pimiento cutouts and fronds of dill in aspic in bottom of mold; spoon several tablespoons of liquid aspic over decorations. Chill again until sticky-firm.

5 Chill remaining gelatin mixture until as thick as unbeaten egg white in bowl of ice and water to speed setting. Stir in drained shrimp and cucumber mixture; gently spoon over decorated layer in ring mold; chill until firm, at least 4 hours. (Overnight is best.)

6 Just before serving, loosen salad around edges with a knife; dip mold *very quickly* in and out of hot water; wipe off water. Cover pan with serving plate; turn upside down; shake gently; lift off mold. Border with reserved cucumber slices, halved. Serve with lettuce leaves and fronds of dill, if you wish. Top with CREAMY DRESSING.

CREAMY DRESSING—Combine ½ cup dairy sour cream; ½ cup mayonnaise or salad dressing; ½ teaspoon salt; ¼ teaspoon celery seed, crushed; and ¼ teaspoon dry mustard in a small bowl; stir to blend well. Cover; refrigerate at least 1 hour to blend flavors. Makes about 1 cup.

Boeuf à la Mode en Gelée

The name is fancy and so is this main-dish salad

Makes 6 servings

- 3 medium carrots, pared and cut in ½-inch slices
- 1 pint Brussels sprouts, washed and trimmed
- 2 cans (10½ ounces each) condensed beef broth
- 1⅓ cups water
- 2 envelopes unflavored gelatin
- 3 tablespoons Madeira or dry sherry
- 6 drops liquid red pepper seasoning
- 1 pound cooked roast beef or steak, sliced thin
- Watercress
- HORSERADISH DRESSING (recipe follows)

1 Cook carrots and Brussels sprouts separately in boiling salted water 15 minutes or until tender. Drain; chill.

2 Combine beef broth and water in medium-size bowl. Soften gelatin in 1 cup of broth, about 5 minutes, in a small saucepan. Heat, stirring constantly, until gelatin dissolves; stir into remaining broth in bowl. Add Madeira or sherry and red pepper seasoning. Cut Brussels sprouts in half lengthwise.

3 Pour ¾ cup of the gelatin mixture into an 11x7x1½-inch pan or an 8-cup shallow mold; place in a larger pan of ice and water until gelatin is sticky-firm Arrange part of the Brussels sprouts and carrots in decorative pattern along sides of pan. Make 12 rolls or bundles of meat slices; place 6 down center of pan, spacing evenly; spoon several tablespoons of remaining gelatin mixture over vegetables and meat. Arrange some of remaining Brussels sprouts against sides of pan. Add enough gelatin mixture to almost cover meat. Chill until sticky-firm.

4 Arrange remaining meat and vegetables on top of first layer in pan; set pan on shelf in refrigerator; carefully spoon remaining gelatin over to cover meat and vegetables completely. Chill until firm, several hours or overnight.

5 Just before serving, loosen gelatin around edges with a knife; dip pan quickly in and out of hot water; wipe off water. Cover pan with serving plate; turn upside down; shake gently; lift off mold. Border with watercress, if you wish. Serve with HORSERADISH DRESSING.

HORSERADISH DRESSING—Combine ¾ cup mayonnaise or salad dressing; 1 hard-cooked egg, sieved; 1 tablespoon tarragon vinegar; and 1 teaspoon prepared horseradish in a small bowl; stir to blend well. Cover; refrigerate to blend flavors. Makes 1 cup.

Molded Corned-Beef Ring

Three favorites—corned beef, cabbage and potatoes—go fancy in this summery salad

Makes 6 servings

Corned-Beef Layer

- 2 envelopes unflavored gelatin
- 2 tablespoons sugar
- 3 cups water
- 2 beef-bouillon cubes
- ½ cup cider vinegar
- 2 cups diced cooked corned beef

MOLDED SALAD RICHES • 33

2 cups chopped celery
¼ cup chopped green pepper
1 tablespoon prepared horseradish

Potato-Salad Layer

4 cups diced, peeled, cooked potatoes
2 cups finely shredded cabbage
1 small onion, chopped (¼ cup)
¼ cup chopped parsley
½ cup mayonnaise or salad dressing
½ cup dairy sour cream
1 teaspoon prepared mustard
1 teaspoon salt

1 Make corned-beef layer: Combine gelatin and sugar in a medium-size saucepan; stir in 1 cup of the water and bouillon cubes. Heat, stirring constantly, until gelatin and bouillon cubes dissolve. Remove from heat; stir in remaining 2 cups water and vinegar to mix well.
2 Measure ¾ cup into a small bowl; let stand at room temperature for Step 4. Pour remaining gelatin mixture into a large bowl; chill 30 minutes, or until as thick as unbeaten egg white.
3 Mash canned corned beef lightly with a fork, then stir into thickened gelatin with celery, green pepper and horseradish. Spoon into a 10-cup ring mold; chill just until sticky-firm.
4 While corned-beef layer chills, make potato-salad layer: Combine potatoes, cabbage, onion and parsley in a large bowl. Blend mayonnaise or salad dressing, sour cream, mustard and salt into the ¾ cup gelatin from Step 2; fold into potato mixture.
5 Spoon over sticky-firm corned-beef layer in mold; chill at least 4 hours, or until firm.
6 Just before serving, run a sharp-tip, thin-blade knife around top of mold, then dip mold *very quickly* in and out of a pan of hot water. Invert onto serving plate; carefully lift off mold. Garnish plate with salad greens and serve with additional mayonnaise or salad dressing, if you wish.

Cranberry Crown

It looks so pretty on a party table. The berries literally shine through the shimmering gelatin

Makes 16 servings, ½ cup each

3 packages (3 ounces each) orange-flavor gelatin
2 cups hot water
1 can (1 pound) whole-fruit cranberry sauce
1 cup bottled cranberry-juice cocktail
1 bottle (7 ounces) ginger ale
1 cup chopped celery
½ cup chopped sweet pickles
¼ cup sweet-pickle juice
 Mayonnaise or salad dressing

1 Dissolve gelatin in hot water in large bowl. Break up cranberry sauce in can with a fork; stir into gelatin mixture with cranberry-juice cocktail and ginger ale. Chill until mixture is as thick as unbeaten egg white.
2 Stir in celery, pickles and juice; spoon into an 8-cup ring mold. Chill several hours, or until firm.
3 To unmold, run a sharp-tip, thin-blade knife around top of mold, then dip *very quickly* in and out of a pan of hot water. Moisten a small cookie sheet with cold water. (This will keep mold from sticking and make it easy to slide onto serving tray later.) Cover mold with cookie sheet; turn upside down, then gently lift off mold. Chill until serving time.
4 Slide mold from cookie sheet onto serving tray, lifting and pushing mold at the same time with a spatula moistened with water. Fill center of ring with a small dish of mayonnaise or salad dressing; garnish with salad greens, if you wish.
Tips for the hostess: Make this mold a day or even two ahead, as it will hold well in the refrigerator.

Buffet Mousse Ring

Lots of chicken and ham, tangy pineapple and crisp water chestnuts go into this rich soufflélike salad mold

Makes 16 servings, ½ cup each

2 large whole chicken breasts (about 2 pounds)
2 cups water
1 small onion, sliced
 Handful of celery tops
1 teaspoon salt
1 bay leaf
4 peppercorns
1 can (about 9 ounces) pineapple chunks
2 envelopes unflavored gelatin
1 tablespoon lemon juice
3 drops liquid red pepper seasoning
1 cup mayonnaise or salad dressing
1 teaspoon prepared mustard
½ pound cooked ham
1 can (5 ounces) water chestnuts, drained

1 Combine chicken breasts, water, onion, celery tops, salt, bay leaf and peppercorns in a

(continued)

34 • MOLDED SALAD RICHES

large saucepan; simmer, covered, 30 minutes, or until chicken is tender.
2 While chicken cooks, drain syrup from pineapple into a 1-cup measure; add water, if needed, to make ½ cup. Stir in gelatin to soften. Set pineapple aside for Steps 8 and 9.
3 Remove chicken from broth; strain broth into a 4-cup measure; add water, if needed, to make 3 cups. Return to same saucepan; stir in softened gelatin.
4 Heat slowly, stirring constantly, until gelatin dissolves; remove from heat. Stir in lemon juice and red pepper seasoning. Measure out ½ cup and set aside for making topping in Step 8. Cool remaining gelatin-mixture in saucepan for Step 6.
5 Slip skin from chicken; remove meat from bones, then dice into small cubes. (There should be about 1½ cups.) Place in a medium-size bowl.
6 Blend mayonnaise or salad dressing and mustard into gelatin in saucepan. Pour into an ice-cube tray; freeze 20 minutes, or just until firm about 1 inch in from edges.
7 To make the fancy top on mold, set aside enough ham to make twelve 2-inch-long strips, each ¼ inch thick. Otherwise dice all of ham. (There should be about 1½ cups.) Slice water chestnuts very thin. Add chestnuts and diced ham to chicken in bowl.
8 Place an 8-cup ring mold in a bowl or pan partly filled with ice cubes and water to speed chilling. If making a plain top, pour the ½ cup saved gelatin into mold; chill until sticky-firm. To make the fancy top, pour ¼ cup of the saved gelatin into mold; chill until mixture is as thick as unbeaten egg white. Arrange some of the chicken, ham strips, pineapple tidbits and water-chestnut slices in an attractive pattern in gelatin. Spoon remaining ¼ cup gelatin over; chill until sticky-firm.
9 Spoon partly frozen gelatin mixture into a chilled large bowl; beat until thick and fluffy; fold in remaining chicken, ham, pineapple and water chestnuts. Spoon over sticky-firm gelatin layer in mold. Chill several hours, or overnight.
10 To unmold, run a sharp-tip, thin-blade knife around top of mold, then dip *very quickly* in and out of a pan of hot water. Moisten a small cookie sheet with cold water. (This will keep mold from sticking and make it easy to slide onto serving tray later.) Cover mold with cookie sheet; turn upside down, then gently lift off mold. Chill until serving time.
11 Slide mold from cookie sheet onto a flat serving tray, lifting and pushing mold at the same time with a spatula moistened with water. Fill center of ring with salad greens, if you wish.
Tips for the hostess: Don't hesitate to make this mold a day or even two ahead, as it will hold well in the refrigerator. Unmold about an hour before serving to avoid last-minute fussing. This ring, as well as the CRANBERRY CROWN, should be served on a large flat tray or platter.

HOW TO UNMOLD A JELLIED SALAD

1 Be sure salad is firm. Run a knife around top to loosen, then dip mold *very quickly* in and out of hot water. This quick heating is just enough to free the bottom.

2 Set your serving plate upside down on top of mold. Then, holding plate and mold firmly with both hands, flip right side up with a mere twist of the wrists.

3 Lift off mold and your prize is ready to garnish. Another tip: If you moisten plate with water first, you can slide salad easily if it's off center on the plate.

Luncheon Salad

There's more than enough salad to satisfy a luncheon appetite

Makes 6 to 8 servings

- 2 packages lemon-flavor gelatin
- 2 cups hot water
- 1½ cups apple juice
- 2 tablespoons lemon juice
- 2 teaspoons prepared horseradish
- ¼ teaspoon salt
- ½ small cucumber, unpared
- ¼ cup diced celery
- ¼ cup thinly sliced radishes
- 1½ cups diced cooked ham

1 Dissolve gelatin in hot water in medium-size bowl; stir in apple juice, lemon juice, horseradish and salt; chill until slightly thickened.
2 Cut cucumber lengthwise into quarters; remove seeds; cut crosswise into thin slices (makes about ½ cup).
3 Combine cucumber, celery, radishes and ham in medium-size bowl; fold into thickened gelatin.
4 Pour into 8-cup mold; chill 4 hours, or until firm.
5 Unmold onto serving plate; garnish with salad greens and radish roses, if desired; serve with your favorite salad dressing.

Cape Cod Cranberry Salad

Two-step salad; good as individual salad or as accompaniment to main-dish meals

Makes 8 servings

- 1 can (8¼ ounces) pineapple chunks
- 1 package (3 ounces) red-cherry-flavor gelatin
- 1 can (1 pound) jellied cranberry sauce
- ¼ cup lemon juice
- 1 carton (8 ounces) cream-style cottage cheese
- ½ cup thinly sliced celery
- ½ cup coarsely broken walnuts
- Romaine

1 Drain syrup from pineapple into a 1-cup measure; add water to make 1 cup. Heat to boiling in a small saucepan; stir into gelatin in a medium-size bowl until gelatin dissolves. Beat in cranberry sauce and lemon juice. Chill 45 minutes, or until as thick as unbeaten egg white.
2 Stir in pineapple, cottage cheese, celery, and walnuts; spoon into a 6-cup mold. Chill several hours, or until firm (overnight is best).
3 When ready to serve, loosen salad around edge with a knife; dip mold *very quickly* in and out of hot water. Cover with a serving plate; turn upside down; gently lift off mold.
4 Garnish with romaine leaves. Serve plain, or with mayonnaise or salad dressing, if you wish.

Tangerine Sunshine Mold

Bursting with color and sweet to the taste

Makes 8 servings

- 2 envelopes unflavored gelatin
- ¼ cup sugar
- ¾ teaspoon salt
- 2 cups water
- 1 can (6 ounces) frozen concentrated tangerine juice
- 3 tablespoons lemon juice
- 1 can (1 pound, 4 ounces) pineapple chunks, drained
- ½ cup grated pared raw carrot

1 Soften gelatin with sugar and salt in one cup of the water in a medium-size saucepan; heat, stirring constantly, until gelatin dissolves; remove from heat.
2 Stir in remaining water, concentrated tangerine and lemon juices. Chill until as thick as unbeaten egg white.
3 Fold in pineapple and carrot; spoon into a 6-cup mold. Chill several hours, or until firm.
4 Unmold onto a serving plate; serve with your favorite mayonnaise or salad dressing, if you wish.

Sun-Gold Egg Mold

Hard-cooked egg slices in shimmering gelatin top zippy egg salad for this luncheon treat

Makes 6 servings

- 1 envelope unflavored gelatin
- ¼ cup water
- 1 can (13¾ ounces) chicken broth
- 1 teaspoon Worcestershire sauce
- 2 pimientos (from a 4-ounce can)
- 5 hard-cooked eggs, shelled
- ½ cup diced celery
- 1 teaspoon grated onion
- ¾ cup mayonnaise or salad dressing
- 2 tablespoons lemon juice
- 1 teaspoon salt

(continued)

MOLDED SALAD RICHES

1 Soften gelatin in water in a small saucepan; heat over low heat, stirring constantly, just until gelatin dissolves. Stir in chicken broth and Worcestershire sauce. Chill 50 minutes, or until as thick as unbeaten egg white.
2 Cut 6 one-inch-long strips of pimiento; arrange, petal fashion, in the bottom of a 4-cup mold. Chop remaining pimiento; set aside for Step 4.
3 Spoon 1 cup of the thickened gelatin over pimiento in mold. Slice 2 of the hard-cooked eggs lengthwise; press 6 of the prettiest slices into gelatin around side of mold. Chill again until sticky-firm.
4 While gelatin chills, chop remaining whole eggs and slices; place in a medium-size bowl with chopped pimiento, celery, onion, mayonnaise or salad dressing, lemon juice, and salt. Mix well, then fold in remaining thickened gelatin.
5 Spoon over sticky-firm layer in mold. Chill until firm.
6 Unmold onto a serving plate. Frame with cucumber slices, if you wish.

When you're stumped for a new salad idea, let **Sun-Gold Egg Mold** take care of your problem.

Jellied Chicken Loaf

A perfect keeper, and wonderfully cool eating on a blistery-hot day.

Makes 6 servings

1 broiler-fryer (about 2½ pounds)
Few celery leaves
1 small onion, sliced
2 teaspoons salt
1 teaspoon ground ginger
8 peppercorns
2 cups water (for chicken)
1 envelope unflavored gelatin
¼ cup cold water (for gelatin)
¼ cup mayonnaise or salad dressing
2 teaspoons soy sauce
½ cup finely diced celery
2 tablespoons finely chopped walnuts

1 Place chicken, celery leaves, onion, salt, ginger, peppercorns, and the 2 cups water in a large saucepan; cover. Heat to boiling, then simmer 1 hour, or until chicken is tender.
2 Remove from broth; cool while fixing gelatin mixture. Strain broth into a 2-cup measure; add water, if needed, to make 2 cups; return to same saucepan.
3 Soften gelatin in the ¼ cup cold water in a 1-cup measure; stir into broth. Heat, stirring

MOLDED SALAD RICHES • 37

As fancy as they come, **Shrimp-Cucumber Diadem** will have guests marveling at your handiwork.

constantly, just until gelatin dissolves; stir in mayonnaise or salad dressing and soy sauce.
4 Pour into a 6-cup bowl or mold; chill until as thick as unbeaten egg white.
5 While gelatin mixture chills, remove chicken from bones; chop meat very fine. (There should be about 2¼ cups.) Stir into chilled gelatin mixture with celery and walnuts. Chill several hours, or until firm.
6 Just before serving, run a sharp-tip, thin-blade knife around top of bowl or mold, then dip bowl *very quickly* in and out of a pan of hot water. Invert onto serving plate; carefully lift off bowl. Garnish with crisp lettuce and sliced tomatoes, and serve with crusty French bread or toasted hard rolls.

Shrimp-Cucumber Diadem

It's a refreshingly cool two-layer salad with a sparkling crown. Serve with marinated shrimps and hot rolls

Makes 6 servings

Shrimp Layer

1 bag (1½ pounds) frozen, deveined, shelled, raw shrimps
3 tablespoons bottled Italian-style salad dressing
1 tablespoon chopped parsley
1 envelope unflavored gelatin
2 envelopes instant chicken broth
 OR: 2 envelopes instant vegetable broth
2 cups water
1 teaspoon grated onion
 Few drops liquid red pepper seasoning
1 large cucumber

Cucumber Layer

1 package (3 ounces) lime-flavor gelatin
1 teaspoon salt
1 cup hot water
2 tablespoons cider vinegar
1 cup dairy sour cream
¼ cup mayonnaise or salad dressing
 TOMATO TOPPERS (recipe follows)

1 Make shrimp layer: Cook shrimps, following label directions; drain. Set aside about 12 for Step 5. Place remaining in a medium-size bowl; add Italian dressing and parsley; toss lightly. Cover and chill until serving time.
2 Soften unflavored gelatin with chicken or vegetable broth in 1 cup of the water in a medium-size saucepan; heat, stirring constantly, just until gelatin dissolves. Stir in remaining 1 cup water, onion, and red-pepper seasoning. Let stand at room temperature for layering mold in Step 5.
3 Score cucumber rind with a fork for about a quarter of its length, then slice scored part *very thin* and halve each slice. Set aside for making fancy topping in Step 5. Pare remainder of the cucumber; chop—seeds and all—then measure. (There should be about 1¼ cups to use in cucumber layer in Step 6.)
4 Start cucumber layer: Dissolve lime gelatin and salt in the 1 cup hot water in a medium-size bowl; stir in vinegar. Chill about 20 minutes, or until gelatin is as thick as unbeaten egg white.

(continued)

38 • MOLDED SALAD RICHES

5 Make fancy topping this way: Set a 6-cup tube mold in a larger bowl or pan partly filled with ice and water to speed setting. Pour ½ cup chicken-broth mixture from Step 2 into mold; chill 5 minutes, or until sticky-soft. Stand halved cucumber slices, rind side down, in gelatin to form a pattern; carefully spoon 1 cup of remaining chicken-broth mixture over. Chill until sticky-firm. Press saved 12 shrimps into gelatin around edge of mold; pour in remaining ½ cup chicken-broth mixture. Chill until sticky-firm.
6 Finish cucumber layer: Blend sour cream and mayonnaise or salad dressing into thickened lime gelatin from Step 4; fold in chopped cucumber. Spoon over shrimp layer in mold. Remove mold from ice and water. Chill at least 3 hours, or until firm. (Overnight is even better.)
7 Just before serving, run a sharp-tip, thin-blade knife around top of mold, then dip mold *very quickly* in and out of a pan of hot water. Invert onto serving plate; carefully lift off mold. Garnish with TOMATO TOPPERS. Serve with marinated shrimps in a separate bowl.
Note: This recipe can be doubled perfectly to make 12 party servings. Make it in a 12-cup mold.

TOMATO TOPPERS—Remove stems from firm cherry tomatoes, allowing one for each serving. Using a sharp-tip, thin-blade knife, score blossom ends halfway down tomato, just through skin, making 5 or 6 cuts; place in a small bowl. Pour boiling water over; let stand 1 minute, then drain. Carefully peel back skin to make petals; top each tomato with a ripe-olive dot. Place on a wooden pick, then stick pick into a lemon wedge.

HOW TO MAKE A JELLIED MOLD

Mixing—Follow directions when dissolving gelatin, as mixture should be sparkling-smooth, with no tiny granules clinging to bowl.

Fruit-flavor gelatin dissolves quickly in hot water. Unflavored gelatin can be dissolved either of these two ways: (1) Soften in cold water, then dissolve in a hot liquid or heat softened gelatin over hot water (as in a double boiler) until dissolved; or (2) mix dry gelatin with sugar, then add liquid and heat, following recipe directions.

Chilling—Place dissolved gelatin in the refrigerator to chill until syrupy-thick (consistency should be like an unbeaten egg white). Gelatin sets first at the bottom and sides of bowl, so stir occasionally for even thickening.

In a hurry? Follow suggestions on package label or hasten setting either of these ways: (1) Pour gelatin mixture into a shallow pan and place in refrigerator; or (2) set bowl of gelatin mixture in a larger bowl of ice and water. Keep on the kitchen counter where you can watch it, as it jells fast.

Gelatin get away from you and set too quickly? Place bowl over simmering water and heat, stirring constantly, until melted. Then start chilling again, as if freshly mixed.

Layering—Like a fancy design on top? Place mold in a larger pan of ice and water (pan should be deep enough so ice and water will come to within one inch of top of mold). Spoon about a ¼-inch-thick layer of syrupy gelatin into a mold and chill just until beginning to be sticky-firm. Arrange foods to make the design you wish on top; carefully spoon in another thin gelatin layer barely to cover; chill just until sticky-firm. This is important whenever you add one layer on top of another.

Make any remaining layers this way: Keep rest of gelatin syrupy-thick. (On a cool day keep at room temperature, or watch it if it is necessary to keep it refrigerated.) Fold in other recipe ingredients, then spoon mixture carefully on top of already-set layer while it is still sticky-firm.

Setting—Place mold in a far corner of your refrigerator where it can chill without being disturbed. Large ones, or those heavy with fruits or vegetables, need at least 12 hours' chilling. Usually small molds are firm enough to turn out after 3 to 4 hours' chilling.

MOLDED SALAD RICHES • 39

Redcap Veal Mousse

Tomato-aspic layer atop creamy-light veal salad makes this most inviting main dish

Makes 6 to 8 servings

Tomato-Aspic Layer

1 envelope unflavored gelatin
1 cup water
1 can (8 ounces) tomato sauce
1 teaspoon lemon juice

Veal Layer

1 envelope unflavored gelatin
1 cup water
1 can (10¾ ounces) condensed cream of celery soup
¼ cup mayonnaise or salad dressing
2 cups chopped cooked veal
¼ cup chopped toasted almonds (from a 5-ounce can)
1 tablespoon chopped parsley
1 teaspoon chopped chives

1 Make tomato-aspic layer: Soften gelatin in water in a small saucepan; heat, stirring constantly, just until gelatin dissolves; remove from heat.
2 Blend in tomato sauce and lemon juice; pour into an 8-cup mold; chill just until sticky-firm.
3 While tomato-aspic layer chills, make veal layer: Soften gelatin in water in a medium-size saucepan; heat, stirring constantly, just until gelatin dissolves. Stir in soup until mixture is smooth; remove from heat.
4 Blend in mayonnaise or salad dressing, then stir in veal, almonds, parsley, and chives. Chill until as thick as unbeaten egg white.
5 Spoon over tomato-aspic layer in mold; chill several hours, or until firm.
6 Just before serving, run a sharp-tip, thin-blade knife around top of mold, then dip mold *very quickly* in and out of a pan of hot water. Invert onto serving plate; carefully lift off mold. Garnish with lemon wedges, and serve with additional mayonnaise or salad dressing, if you wish.

Perfection Cheese Loaf

A vegetable salad with a cottage cheese topping

Makes 8 servings

2 packages (3 ounces each) lime-flavor gelatin
2 cups hot water
1¾ cups cold water
4 tablespoons lemon juice
½ cup finely shredded cabbage
½ cup chopped celery
½ cup shredded carrots
¼ cup thinly sliced radishes
2 cups (2 eight-ounce containers) cottage cheese
1 teaspoon grated onion
¼ teaspoon salt

1 Dissolve gelatin in hot water; stir in cold water and lemon juice; divide in half; chill one half until syrupy; keep other half at room temperature for Step 3.
2 Fold vegetables into syrupy gelatin; pour into 8-cup mold; chill until firm.
3 Chill second half of gelatin until syrupy; fold in cottage cheese combined with grated onion and salt; spoon over chilled layer in mold; chill until firm.
4 Unmold onto platter; garnish with radish roses and watercress.

Molded Carrot Cups

The soft blending of green peppers, carrots, and chicory provide the secret to this easy-to-do salad mold

Makes 12 servings

2 packages (6 ounces each) lemon-flavor gelatin
4 cups boiling water
2 cups cold water
½ cup cider vinegar
¾ cup finely diced green pepper
2 cups shredded carrots
Chicory or curly endive
Mayonnaise or salad dressing

1 Dissolve gelatin in boiling water in a large bowl; stir in cold water and vinegar. Measure 1½ cups of mixture into a small bowl for next step. Keep remaining gelatin mixture at room temperature while layering molds.
2 Place small bowl in a pan of ice and water to speed setting. Chill until as thick as unbeaten egg white; fold in green pepper. Spoon into 12 five-ounce custard cups. Chill in refrigerator just until sticky-firm.

(continued)

MOLDED SALAD RICHES

3 While molds chill, place bowl of remaining gelatin mixture in ice and water. Chill just until as thick as unbeaten egg white; fold in carrots. Spoon over pepper layers in molds. Chill at least 4 hours, or until firm. (Overnight is best.)
4 When ready to serve, unmold onto salad plates. Garnish with chicory or curly endive and top each with mayonnaise or salad dressing.

Ginger-Orange Mold

Everyone will love this side-dish salad

Makes 6 servings

1 package (3 ounces) lemon-flavor gelatin
½ teaspoon onion powder
¼ teaspoon ground ginger
1 cup boiling water
1 can (11 ounces) mandarin-orange segments
    Cold water
1 can (5 ounces) water chestnuts, drained and sliced thin

1 Combine gelatin, onion powder, and ginger in a medium-size bowl; stir in boiling water until gelatin dissolves.
2 Drain syrup from mandarin-orange segments into a 1-cup measure; add cold water to make 1 cup; stir into gelatin mixture. Chill about 45 minutes, or until as thick as unbeaten egg white. Fold in orange segments and water chestnuts; pour into a 4-cup mold. Chill several hours, or until firm.
3 When ready to serve, unmold onto a serving plate. Frame base with chicory or curly endive, if you wish.

There's more flavor to **Ginger-Orange Mold** than the eye would suspect.

Curried-Chicken Coronet

A partylike rich chicken-salad mousse delicately spiced with curry

Makes 8 servings

2 whole chicken breasts (about 2 pounds)
2 cups water
1 medium-size onion, sliced
    Handful of celery tops
1 teaspoon salt (for chicken)
3 peppercorns
1 envelope unflavored gelatin
2 eggs, separated
½ cup chopped toasted almonds
1 teaspoon curry powder
½ teaspoon salt (for salad)
¼ teaspoon pepper
1 cup mayonnaise or salad dressing
1 cup cream for whipping
1 can (about 13 ounces) frozen pineapple chunks, thawed and drained
½ cup flaked coconut

1 Combine chicken breasts, water, onion, celery tops, 1 teaspoon salt and peppercorns in large saucepan; simmer, covered, 45 minutes, or until chicken is tender. Let stand until cool enough to handle, then skin chicken and take meat from bones. Dice chicken fine (you should have about 2 cups).
2 Strain stock into a bowl; measure out 1 cupful; pour into a medium-size saucepan and cool. (Use any remaining stock for soup for another day.)
3 Soften gelatin in cooled stock in saucepan; heat, stirring constantly, just until dissolved.
4 Beat egg yolks slightly in small bowl; slowly stir in dissolved gelatin. Return mixture to saucepan and cook, stirring constantly, 1 minute, or until slightly thickened; remove from heat.
5 Stir in diced chicken, almonds, curry powder, ½ teaspoon salt and pepper, blending well. Chill 30 minutes, or until mixture is syrupy thick; blend in mayonnaise or salad dressing.
6 Beat egg whites until stiff in large bowl; fold in chicken mixture until no streaks of white remain.
7 Beat cream until stiff in medium-size bowl; fold into chicken mixture.
8 Pour into a 6-cup ring mold; chill several hours, or until firm.
9 Unmold onto serving plate; fit a shallow bowl into center of mold; fill with drained pineapple chunks; sprinkle with coconut.

One of the secrets to a good table is color appeal. The happy combination of **Curried-Chicken Coronet** and **Rainbow Fruit Mold** is a good example.

Rainbow Fruit Mold

Three color-bright layers, each with a tangy fruit, make this a handsome salad-dessert

Makes 8 to 12 servings

- 1 package (3 ounces) lemon-flavor gelatin
- 1 package (3 ounces) strawberry-flavor gelatin
- 1 package (3 ounces) orange-flavor gelatin
- 3 cups hot water
- 2¼ cups cold water
- ½ cup drained canned sliced peaches (from an 8-ounce can)
- 1 cup sliced ripe firm strawberries
- 1 can (about 11 ounces) mandarin-orange sections, drained
- 1 cup cream for whipping

1 Mix and chill each fruit-flavor gelatin, one at a time and 15 minutes apart, this way: Start with lemon-flavor gelatin, then strawberry and then orange; dissolve each in 1 cup hot water in a shallow pan, then stir ¾ cup cold water into each; chill until syrupy-thick. (The time intervals of 15 minutes are important so all gelatins do not become syrupy at once.)

2 As soon as lemon gelatin is syrupy-thick, place an 8-cup bowl (we used a kitchen mixing bowl) in a larger bowl of ice and water; pour ½ cup syrupy gelatin into bowl and make a design of peach slices on top.

(continued)

MOLDED SALAD RICHES

3 Let layer set a few minutes, or until sticky-firm, then gradually spoon ¾ cup more syrupy lemon gelatin over peaches. (Pour remaining ½ cup lemon gelatin into orange-flavor gelatin that is chilling. This will make all layers look of equal depth when mold is turned out.) Let lemon-peach layer set until sticky-firm, keeping bowl in bowl of ice until all layers have been added.
4 Next, fold sliced strawberries into syrupy strawberry gelatin; carefully spoon on top of sticky-firm lemon-peach layer in bowl, pushing some berries to edge so fruit will show when unmolded; let stand until sticky-firm.
5 Fold mandarin-orange sections into orange-gelatin mixture; carefully spoon into mold, pushing some sections to edge; don't move until set, as bowl is filled to the top (add ice if needed). Remove bowl from ice water; chill overnight, or until very firm.
6 Beat cream until stiff in medium-size bowl. Unmold gelatin onto serving plate; top with some whipped cream; serve remaining to spoon over.

Buffet Mold

As the name suggests, let this mold star on a buffet

Makes 6 to 8 servings

- 2 envelopes unflavored gelatin
- 2¾ cups cold water
- 1 can (6 ounces) frozen concentrated orange juice
- ¼ cup sugar
- ⅛ teaspoon salt
- 2 tablespoons lemon juice
- ½ cup shredded carrot
- ½ cup finely chopped celery
- 1 cup cottage cheese
- 1 can (8¼ ounces) crushed pineapple, drained

1 Soften gelatin in ½ cup cold water in top of double boiler; dissolve over hot water; remove from heat.
2 Stir in orange juice, 2¼ cups water, sugar, salt and lemon juice; divide in half; chill one half until syrupy; keep other half at room temperature for Step 4.
3 Fold carrot and celery into syrupy gelatin; pour into 6-cup mold; chill until almost set. (Gelatin layer should be slightly sticky so second layer will mold to it as it chills.)
4 Chill second half of gelatin until syrupy; fold in cottage cheese and pineapple; spoon carefully on top of almost-firm gelatin; chill 2 to 3 hours, or until firm. Unmold; serve plain or with dressing.

Tomato-Aspic Crown

Tartly seasoned relish in a no-fuss aspic ring to go with the chicken-salad mold

Makes 8 servings

- 3 envelopes unflavored gelatin
- 3 cups water
- 3 cans (8 ounces each) tomato sauce
- 1 tablespoon lemon juice
  FRESH VEGETABLE RELISH (recipe follows)

1 Soften gelatin in 1 cup water in medium-size saucepan; heat slowly, stirring constantly, just until dissolved. Stir in remaining 2 cups water, tomato sauce and lemon juice.
2 Pour into a 6-cup ring mold; chill several hours, or until firm.
3 Unmold onto serving plate; fill center with FRESH VEGETABLE RELISH.
  FRESH VEGETABLE RELISH—Wash and stem 2 cups (1 pint) cherry tomatoes. Combine with 1 cup sliced crisp celery, 1 cup diced green pepper and 1 cup coarsely chopped Bermuda onion in a large bowl. Drizzle with ⅓ cup lemon juice; toss lightly. Chill at least 1 hour. Makes about 4 cups.

Cucumber-Cream Mold

Go spicy with this semi-hot salad

Makes 6 servings

- 1 package (3 ounces) lemon-flavor gelatin
- ¾ cup hot water
- ½ cup cold water
- 2 tablespoons lemon juice
- 1 teaspoon salt
- ⅛ teaspoon pepper
- 1 medium-size cucumber
- 2 medium-size carrots, pared

MOLDED SALAD RICHES • 43

1 ripe olive
1 tablespoon chopped parsley
1 teaspoon grated onion
1 cup dairy sour cream
  Watercress

1 Dissolve gelatin in hot water in medium-size bowl; stir in cold water, lemon juice, salt and pepper. Spoon a thin layer into 4-cup mold or dish; set mold in larger pan of ice and water to speed setting. Chill until just beginning to be sticky-firm. (Keep remaining gelatin at room temperature.)
2 Slice half the cucumber very thin; arrange slices, overlapping, in ring on sticky-firm gelatin in mold. Cut 5 thin slices from a carrot and 1 slice from ripe olive; arrange in center of cucumber ring to make a flower design. Carefully spoon in another thin layer of gelatin; let set until sticky-firm.
3 Pare and chop remaining cucumber and grate carrots into small bowl. Stir in parsley and onion, then sour cream; fold into remaining gelatin. Spoon over chilled gelatin in mold; remove from ice; chill until firm.
4 Unmold by first loosening around edge with thin-blade knife, then dipping quickly in and out of a pan of hot water. Invert onto serving plate; garnish with watercress.

Boston Beanie Ring

Summertime's picnic favorite puts on molded salad airs. Serve with frankfurters or grilled hamburgers

Makes 6 servings

1 cup tomato juice
1 package (3 ounces) lemon-flavor gelatin
⅓ cup catsup
3 tablespoons lemon juice
1 teaspoon prepared mustard
½ teaspoon salt
1 can (1 pound) baked beans in tomato sauce
½ cup diced celery
¼ cup drained sweet-pickle relish
  Small inner romaine leaves

1 Heat tomato juice to boiling in a small saucepan; pour over gelatin in a medium-size bowl; stir until gelatin dissolves.
2 Stir in catsup, lemon juice, mustard and salt. Chill 30 minutes, or until as thick as unbeaten egg white.

It looks inviting and **Boston Beanie Ring** is as good as it looks.

3 Fold in baked beans, celery and pickle relish; spoon into a 5-cup ring mold. Chill several hours, or until firm. (Overnight is best.)
4 When ready to serve, run a sharp-tip thin-blade knife around top of salad, then dip mold *very quickly* in and out of a pan of hot water. Cover mold with a serving plate; turn upside down; carefully lift off mold. Stand romaine leaves in center of ring.

Aspic-Bean Molds

Green beans give individual jellied tomato salads a different flavor lift

Makes 6 servings

1 envelope unflavored gelatin
2 cups tomato juice
2 tablespoons lemon juice
  Few drops liquid red pepper seasoning
½ teaspoon salt
1 cup crisply cooked cut green beans
  Iceberg lettuce
1½ teaspoons mayonnaise or salad dressing

1 Soften gelatin in ½ cup of the tomato juice in a medium-size saucepan; heat slowly, stirring constantly until gelatin dissolves; remove from heat. Stir in remaining tomato juice, lemon juice, liquid red pepper seasoning and salt. Chill until as thick as unbeaten egg white.
2 Fold in green beans; spoon into 6 individual molds or 5-ounce custard cups. Chill several hours, or until firm. When ready to serve, unmold onto lettuce-lined plates. Top each with mayonnaise or salad dressing.

Coleslaw-Relish Mold

This is a mold you crunch on—and each bite is satisfying

Makes 6 servings

- 2 packages (3 ounces each) lemon-flavor gelatin
- 2 cups boiling water
- 1½ cups cold water
- ½ cup finely shredded green pepper
- 1 cup finely shredded pared carrot
- ⅔ cup mayonnaise or salad dressing
- 2 tablespoons sugar
- ¼ teaspoon salt
- 3 tablespoons milk
- 4 teaspoons cider vinegar
- 3 cups coarsely shredded cabbage
- Chicory or curly endive

1 Dissolve gelatin in boiling water in a medium-size bowl; stir in cold water. Measure ½ cup into a 6-cup mold and set aside for next step. Measure 1 cup into a small bowl. Chill gelatin mixture in medium-size bowl 30 minutes, and gelatin mixture in small bowl 20 minutes, or until as thick as unbeaten egg white.
2 Place mold in a pan of ice and water to speed setting. Chill layer until as thick as unbeaten egg white; stir in green pepper. Continue chilling *just* until sticky-firm.
3 Stir carrot into thickened gelatin in small bowl; spoon over pepper layer in mold. Chill *just* until sticky-firm.
4 While carrot layer chills, beat mayonnaise or salad dressing, sugar, salt, milk and vinegar into thickened gelatin in medium-size bowl; fold in cabbage; spoon over carrot layer in mold. Remove from ice and water. Chill in refrigerator 6 hours, or until firm.
5 Unmold onto a serving plate; frame with chicory or endive leaves. Garnish mold with several green-pepper "petals" and a carrot curl threaded onto a wooden pick.

Lemon Beet Mold

The parsley dressing adds a distinctive flavor to this favorite

Makes 6 servings

- 1 package (3 ounces) lemon-flavor gelatin
- 1 cup boiling water
- 1 cup cold water
- 2 tablespoons lemon juice
- 1 can (1 pound) diced beets, drained
- ¼ cup chopped green onions
- PARSLEY DRESSING (recipe follows)

1 Dissolve gelatin in boiling water in a medium-size bowl; stir in cold water and lemon juice. Chill 50 minutes, or just until as thick as unbeaten egg white.
2 Fold in beets and onions; spoon into a 4-cup mold. Chill several hours, or until firm.
3 Unmold onto a serving plate; garnish with romaine, if you wish, and serve with PARSLEY DRESSING.

PARSLEY DRESSING—Blend ½ cup mayonnaise or salad dressing with 2 tablespoons cream and 2 tablespoons chopped parsley in a small bowl.

Madrilène Cups

Layers of paper-thin vegetable slices seem to float in this shimmering first-course salad

Makes 6 servings

- 1 envelope unflavored gelatin
- 1½ cups water
- 1 chicken-bouillon cube
- 1 can (12 ounces) jellied madrilène
- 6 small radishes, thinly sliced
- 1 small cucumber, thinly sliced
- 1 medium-size carrot, pared and thinly sliced
- 6 thin slices of lime

1 Soften gelatin in 1 cup water in small saucepan; add bouillon cube. Heat, stirring constantly, until gelatin and cube are dissolved.
2 Remove from heat; stir in remaining ½ cup water and madrilène; chill 1 hour, or until syrupy-thick.
3 Place 6 six-ounce custard cups or molds in a shallow pan of ice and water. Spoon 1 tablespoon syrupy gelatin into each cup; let set until just beginning to be sticky-firm, then arrange a layer of sliced radishes, overlapping, in gelatin. Carefully spoon in 2 tablespoons more syrupy gelatin, and again let set until sticky-firm.
4 Repeat, making a layer of cucumber slices and 2 tablespoons syrupy gelatin, then one of carrot slices and 3 tablespoons syrupy gelatin for each. Remove from pan of ice and water and chill until firm.

MOLDED SALAD RICHES • 45

5 Unmold onto serving dishes; garnish each with a twist of sliced lime. Serve plain, or with a cut stalk of Belgian endive and crisp crackers, if you wish.

Raspberry Chiffon Royale

Serve this double-tier pink party special with your favorite cookies

Makes 8 to 12 servings

- 1 envelope unflavored gelatin
- ¾ cup sugar
- ½ cup water
- 4 eggs, separated
- 1 can (6 ounces) frozen concentrate for raspberry-lemon punch or pink lemonade
- 1 cup cream for whipping
    Red food coloring
    Fresh red raspberries

1 Mix gelatin with ½ cup sugar in top of small double boiler (save remaining ¼ cup sugar for Step 4); stir in water.
2 Beat egg yolks slightly in small bowl; stir into gelatin mixture. Cook over simmering water, stirring constantly, 5 minutes, or until gelatin is dissolved and mixture coats a metal spoon.
3 Remove from heat; pour into large bowl; stir in frozen concentrate until completely melted.
4 Beat egg whites until foamy in medium-size bowl; gradually beat in remaining ¼ cup sugar, a tablespoon at a time, until meringue forms soft peaks. Fold into gelatin mixture.
5 Beat cream until stiff in same bowl, then fold into gelatin-meringue mixture until no streaks of white remain.
6 Tint mixture pale pink with a few drops of red food coloring, then measure out 2 cups and tint a deeper pink with a drop or two more.
7 Spoon deeper-pink mixture into an 8-cup mold; chill 15 minutes, or just until sticky-firm. Spoon remaining lighter-pink mixture on top; chill several hours, or until firm.
8 Unmold onto serving plate; garnish top with crown of fresh raspberries.

Lemon Berry Mold

Serve this salad-dessert with a tangy-sweet topper

Makes 6 servings

- 2 envelopes unflavored gelatin
- 1 cup sugar
- ½ teaspoon salt
- 3½ cups water
- ½ cup lemon juice
    Yellow food coloring
- 1 pint strawberries, washed and stemmed
    CHEESE FLUFF (recipe follows)

(continued)

Let the mystery of a favorite fruit shine as it does in **Raspberry Chiffon Royale.**

5 Unmold onto serving plate; top with saved strawberry. Serve with CHEESE FLUFF.

CHEESE FLUFF—Soften 1 package (3 or 4 ounces) cream cheese in a small bowl. Beat ½ cup cream for whipping with 1 tablespoon sugar until stiff in a second small bowl; fold into cheese. Makes about 1¼ cups.

Jeweled Honeydew Mold

Thin melon crescents and strawberries shine through rosy gelatin for this salad-dessert to serve with a creamy lemon topper

Makes 8 servings

1 package (6 ounces) strawberry-flavor gelatin
1 package (3 ounces) lemon-flavor gelatin
3 cups hot water
2 cups cold water
½ medium-size honeydew melon
½ cup sliced hulled strawberries
½ cup cream for whipping
½ teaspoon vanilla
½ cup lemon sherbet, softened slightly

1 Dissolve strawberry and lemon gelatins in hot water in a large bowl; stir in cold water. Pour ½ cup into a lightly oiled 6-cup bowl. Place bowl in a pan of ice and water to speed setting; chill until softly set. Keep remaining gelatin mixture at room temperature for Step 3.
2 Scoop seeds from honeydew melon; slice half into 8 thin wedges; pare each, then trim off inside of each slice, leaving a band about ¼ inch thick. Dice trimmings and set aside with remaining melon for Steps 4 and 5.
3 Place the 8 melon slices, spoke fashion, in softly set gelatin in bowl so slices meet in center; carefully spoon in another ½ cup gelatin mixture; chill until sticky-firm. Trim top edge of slices even with bowl so salad will stand flat when turned out.
4 While mold chills, chill remaining gelatin mixture in refrigerator 30 minutes, or until as thick as unbeaten egg white; fold in diced honeydew from Step 2 and strawberries; carefully spoon into mold. Remove from pan of ice and water. Chill in refrigerator several hours, or until firm. (Overnight is even better.)
5 Cut balls from remaining melon with a melon-ball cutter or ¼ teaspoon of a measuring-spoon set.
6 When ready to serve, run a sharp-tip thin-blade knife carefully around top of bowl, then dip bowl *quickly* in and out of a pan of hot water.

Make your shimmering dessert extra-special with a fresh fruit garnish.

1 Soften gelatin with sugar and salt in 1 cup of the water in a small saucepan; heat, stirring constantly, just until gelatin dissolves.
2 Pour into a medium-size bowl; stir in remaining 2½ cups water and lemon juice; tint lemon-yellow with food coloring.
3 Make a design on top of mold this way: Pour a one-inch depth of gelatin mixture into a 6-cup mold; chill along with remaining gelatin in bowl until layer is as thick as unbeaten egg white. Arrange a ring of strawberries, pointed ends out, in gelatin in mold; chill until sticky-firm.
4 Fold remaining strawberries, saving one for garnish, into thickened gelatin in bowl; spoon over sticky-firm layer in mold. Chill several hours, or until firm.

Cover with a serving plate; turn upside down; carefully lift off bowl. Garnish with melon balls.
7 Beat cream with vanilla until stiff in a small bowl; fold in softened sherbet. Serve separately to spoon over salad.

Party Fruit Tower

Star this frozen beauty as salad and dessert, as it's rich

Makes 8 to 10 servings

- 1 can (1 pound) apricot halves
- 1 can (1 pound) cling-peach slices
- 1 package (3 ounces) strawberry-flavor gelatin
- 1 cup hot water
- 2 tablespoons lemon juice
- 1 package (8 ounces) cream cheese
- ½ cup mayonnaise or salad dressing
- ½ cup cream for whipping
- 1½ cups tiny marshmallows
- ½ cup sliced maraschino cherries

1 Drain syrups from apricots and peaches into a 2-cup measure. Cut fruits into small pieces and set aside for Step 5.
2 Dissolve gelatin in hot water in a 4-cup measure; stir in 1¼ cups of the fruit syrup and lemon juice; cool to lukewarm.
3 Beat cream cheese until soft and smooth in a large bowl; blend in mayonnaise or salad dressing, then gelatin mixture. Set bowl in a pan of ice and water to speed setting. Chill at room temperature, stirring often, just until as thick as unbeaten egg white.
4 While gelatin mixture chills, beat cream until stiff in a small bowl.
5 Fold cut apricots and peaches, marshmallows and cherries into thickened gelatin mixture, then gently fold in whipped cream until mixture starts to mound softly. Spoon into an 8-cup mold. Freeze six hours, or until firm. (Overnight is best.)
6 When ready to serve, run a sharp-tip thin-blade knife around top of salad, then dip mold *very quickly* in and out of a pan of hot water. Cover mold with a serving plate; turn upside down; carefully lift off mold. Garnish salad and plate with watercress or small crisp lettuce leaves, if you wish.

Add contrast to a clear gelatin salad with fruit of a different color.

Summertime is melon-time and what better trio than **Party Melon Bowl** (rear), **Buffet Melon Basket Salad** (right), and **Cantaloupe Fruit Coupe**.

Fruit Salad Spectaculars

What better way to spruce up a summer dining table than with a colorful fruit salad. Whether side-dish or main-dish, a simple or artistically created fruit salad will highlight a table and satisfy the most finicky appetite.

Buffet Melon Basket Salad

A spreading basket filled with fruits of your choosing

Makes 16 servings

½ small watermelon (crosswise cut)
1 cantaloupe, halved and seeded
½ small honeydew melon, seeded
1 large honeydew melon, halved lengthwise, seeded and cut into 16 crescents
Fresh mint
ORANGE-CREAM DRESSING *(recipe follows)*

1 Trim a 1-inch-thick round from cut end of watermelon. Make balls of pink meat with a melon-ball scoop or half teaspoon of a metal measuring-spoon set. Place in a small bowl and save for next step. Trim any remaining meat close to rind, leaving circle of rind whole; save circle for base of "basket" in Step 3.
2 Cut out about 3 cups of balls from remaining watermelon and add to bowl. Cut 2 cups balls from cantaloupe, and 1 cup from the half honeydew. Place in separate bowls; cover; chill until serving time.
3 When ready to serve, place saved circle of rind on a large serving plate. Stand honeydew crescents around inside of circle, so lower ends meet in the center and rind rests against watermelon circle. (Hold ends in place with one hand while putting remaining crescents in place with the other.)
4 Carefully spoon watermelon balls into bottom of basket. Top with layers of cantaloupe and honeydew balls. Garnish with a few sprigs of fresh mint. Serve with ORANGE-CREAM DRESSING.

Orange-Cream Dressing

Makes 2 cups

½ cup sugar
1 teaspoon flour
½ teaspoon dry mustard
¼ teaspoon salt
2 eggs
½ cup orange juice
⅓ cup lemon juice
½ cup cream for whipping

1 Mix sugar, flour, mustard and salt in a cup.
2 Beat eggs slightly in top of a double boiler; blend in dry ingredients, then stir in orange and lemon juices.
3 Cook, stirring constantly, over simmering water, 5 minutes, or until mixture coats a metal spoon. Remove from heat; strain into a medium-size bowl; cover. Chill.
4 Just before serving beat cream until stiff in a small bowl; fold into chilled dressing.

Carolina Melon Salad

A southern specialty that will have them asking for more

Makes 6 to 8 servings

6 cups broken salad greens
1 small cantaloupe, pared, seeded and sliced thin
½ small honeydew melon, pared, seeded and sliced thin
1 lime, sliced thin
GINGER DRESSING *(recipe follows)*

1 Partly fill a large salad bowl with greens; arrange slices of cantaloupe, honeydew and lime, overlapping, in rings on top.
2 Serve with GINGER DRESSING to spoon over. Or layer the melon slices with salad greens in bowl. Drizzle about ¼ cup dressing over; toss to mix and coat greens well. Serve with lime slices. (Save remaining dressing for salad for another meal.)
GINGER DRESSING—Combine ½ cup olive oil or vegetable oil, ¼ cup wine vinegar or cider vinegar, 1 teaspoon sugar, 1 teaspoon celery salt, ½ teaspoon ground ginger, and ¼ teaspoon salt in jar with tight-fitting lid; shake well to mix. Makes about ¾ cup.

Party Watermelon Bowl

A trick with a cookie cutter turns watermelon into a pretty server for ham-chicken salad

Makes 6 servings

1 five-inch piece of watermelon, cut from an end
2 cups diced cooked ham
2 cups diced cooked chicken
2 cups sliced celery
2 tablespoons sweet-pickle relish
1 teaspoon salt
½ cup mayonnaise or salad dressing
½ cup dairy sour cream

1 Place watermelon on a cutting board; trim off rounded end to make bottom flat. Make scallops around top this way: With a 2-inch cookie cutter, cut scallops about ½ inch apart through green skin and white rind to pink meat. Run a sharp knife between rind and meat to separate; lift out cut pieces of rind.
2 Cut a guideline around top in pink meat 1 inch in from green skin. Working inside guideline, cut out about 24 balls with a melon-ball scoop or the half teaspoon of a metal measuring-spoon set to form a shallow bowl. Place balls in a small bowl; cover and chill along with watermelon bowl.
3 Combine ham, chicken, celery, sweet-pickle relish and salt in a medium-size bowl; fold in mayonnaise or salad dressing and sour cream; cover; chill.
4 When ready to serve, place watermelon bowl on a large serving plate. Pile ham-chicken salad in center; circle with watermelon balls; top with 3 or 4 more balls
Note—After serving, cut off top of watermelon bowl and discard. Slice remaining melon as fruit for another meal.

Cantaloupe-Fruit Coupe

This is so sparkling fresh that it would be a pity to drizzle a dressing over it

Makes 6 servings

3 small ripe cantaloupes
2 cups strawberries (1 pint)
2 cups sliced peaches
2 cans (8¼ ounces each) pineapple chunks, drained
1 can (8 ounces) apricot halves, drained
2 bananas, peeled and sliced
½ cup toasted slivered almonds (from a 5-ounce can)
HONEY DRESSING (recipe follows)
10X (confectioners' powdered) sugar

1 Mark a guideline lengthwise around middle of each cantaloupe with tip of knife, then make even saw-tooth cuts into melon above and below line all the way around. Pull halves apart gently; scoop out seeds.
2 Set aside 6 of the prettiest strawberries for next step; slice remaining and combine with peaches, pineapple, apricots, bananas and almonds in a medium-size bowl; fold in HONEY DRESSING.
3 Spoon fruit mixture into cantaloupe halves. Dip tips of saved whole strawberries into 10X sugar; place 1 on top of each salad.
HONEY DRESSING—Combine ¼ cup vegetable oil, 2 tablespoons lemon juice, 1 tablespoon honey, ¼ teaspoon salt and ⅛ teaspoon ground ginger in a jar with tight-fitting lid; shake well to mix; chill. Makes about ½ cup.

Frosted Honeydew Cresents

The honeydew is fresh; pile frosted fruits on top of it just before serving

Makes 8 servings

1 can (1 pound, 13 ounces) fruit cocktail
1 package (3 ounces) strawberry-flavor gelatin
1 cup hot water
2 tablespoons lemon juice
1 package (8 ounces) cream cheese
½ cup mayonnaise or salad dressing
1½ cups tiny marshmallows
½ cup sliced maraschino cherries
½ cup cream for whipping
1 honeydew melon

1 Drain syrup from fruit cocktail into a 2-cup measure to use in next step. Set fruit aside for Step 3.
2 Dissolve gelatin in hot water in a small bowl; stir in 1¼ cups syrup and lemon juice; cool to lukewarm.
3 Soften cream cheese in a large bowl; blend in mayonnaise or salad dressing, then lukewarm gelatin mixture. Fold in fruit cocktail, marshmallows and cherries.
4 Beat cream until stiff in small bowl.
5 Place bowl of fruit-gelatin mixture in a larger bowl or pan partly filled with ice and water; fold

FRUIT SALAD SPECTACULARS • 51

in whipped cream. Continue folding, keeping over ice, 10 minutes, or until mixture starts to mound lightly on a spoon.
6 Pour into 2 ice-cube trays or an 8-cup shallow pan. Freeze 3 hours, or until firm.
7 When ready to serve, cut honeydew into 8 wedges; remove seeds; place wedges on serving plates. Spoon a mound of frozen fruit mixture onto each wedge. (Keep any remaining fruit mixture frozen to serve on lettuce for another meal.)

Sunshine Fruit Salad

A happy combination of melons, oranges, and surprisingly tangy Bermuda oranges

Makes 6 servings

- 4 cups broken salad greens
- 3 cups mixed cantaloupe and honeydew-melon balls
- 2 oranges, peeled and sectioned
- 3 thin slices Bermuda onion, separated into rings
- ¼ cup vegetable oil
- 2 tablespoons cider vinegar
- ½ teaspoon sugar
- ¼ teaspoon salt
- ¼ teaspoon dillweed
- ⅛ teaspoon dry mustard
- ⅛ teaspoon paprika

1 Partly fill a salad bowl with greens; top with melon balls, orange sections and onion rings.
2 Combine remaining ingredients in a jar with tight-fitting lid; shake well.
3 Drizzle half over salad; toss lightly to mix. Pass remaining dressing.

Party Melon Tray

This is a tray you'll feel good about putting on the table

Makes 8 servings

- 2 small honeydew melons
- ¼ watermelon
- 2 limes, sliced thin
- 1 medium-size cantaloupe
- AVOCADO CHIP CREAM (recipe follows)

1 Make honeydew basket this way: Mark a guideline lengthwise around center of one of the melons with the tip of a knife, then mark off an inch-wide strip across top for basket handle. Cut out sections between marks; remove seeds from "basket" and sections, then chill both until ready to arrange tray.
2 Cut 16 balls from watermelon with a small ice-cream scoop or tablespoon of a measuring-spoon set; remove seeds. Cut about a dozen tiny balls from remaining watermelon with a melon-ball scoop or ¼ teaspoon of a measuring-spoon set; chill all.
3 When ready to serve, thread tiny watermelon balls and lime slices on wooden picks; stick into handle of basket. Set basket in center of a large tray.
4 Halve remaining honeydew melon and cantaloupe; remove seeds; slice melons and saved honeydew sections into thin wedges. Arrange around basket on tray. Stack big watermelon balls in a pyramid in front. Spoon AVOCADO CHIP CREAM into basket.

Avocado Chip Cream

The secret lies in blending half the avocado smooth

Makes about 2½ cups

- 1 large ripe avocado
- 1 package (8 ounces) cream cheese
- ½ cup dairy sour cream
- 2 tablespoons lemon juice
- 2 tablespoons honey

1 Halve avocado, then peel and pit. Cut one half into small chunks and place in an electric-blender container. Slice in cream cheese, then add sour cream, lemon juice and honey; cover. Beat at high speed 1 minute, or until smooth. (If you don't have a blender, mash avocado in a medium-size bowl, then beat in remaining ingredients until smooth.)
2 Cut remaining half of avocado into ¼-inch cubes; fold into dressing; cover; chill.

GUIDE TO BUYING FRESH FRUITS

FRUIT	SEASON	MARKS OF QUALITY	AMOUNT NEEDED PER PERSON
Apples	Year round, but supplies are best in fall and winter	Firmness, symmetrical shape; good bright color, no soft spots	1 medium-size
Apricots	June and July	Plumpness, juiciness; uniform golden color	1 to 2 medium-size
Avocados	Year round	Bright green or dark color, no dark spots; slight but uniform softness	½ medium-size
Bananas	Year round	Firmness; bright yellow color without bruises or black spots	1 medium-size
Blueberries	May through September	Plumpness; deep blue color with silvery bloom	½ to ⅔ cup
Blackberries	July to September	Plumpness, juiciness; glossy black color	⅔ to 1 cup
Cantaloupes	May to November	Heavily netted skin, smooth sunken scar at the stem end; sweet aroma	¼ medium-size
Cherries, Sweet	May through August	Dark, rich red color	¼ pound
Cranberries	November through January	Glossy, dark red color; uniform size	¼ pound
Grapefruits	Year round	Waxy skin; firmness, heaviness	½ medium-size
Grapes	June through January with peak supplies in fall	Plump, well-shaped bunches; soft-to-the-touch fruit securely attached to stems	½ pound
Honeydew Melons	June through October	Velvety, pale green skin, slight softness at the blossom end; pleasant bouquet	⅛ to 1/6 medium-size
Lemons	Year round	Firmness, heaviness; waxy yellow skin	
Limes	Year round	Firmness, heaviness; waxy-smooth bright green skin	

FRUIT SALAD SPECTACULARS • 53

FRUIT	SEASON	MARKS OF QUALITY	AMOUNT NEEDED PER PERSON
Nectarines	June through September	Rich peach-to-rose color; plumpness, softness along the seam	1 medium-size
Oranges	Year round	Firmness, heaviness; bright orange or yellow-orange color; waxy or pebbly skin	1 medium-size
Peaches	July to September	Plumpness; rich peach color with blushes of red; softness along the seam; sweet fruity fragrance	1 medium-size
Pears	Autumn and winter	Firmness without hardness; fragrant bouquet; lack of blemishes, bruises or nicks	1 medium-size
Pineapples	Year round	Plumpness, glossy "eyes," good aroma; unblemished, unmoldy appearance	¼ medium-size
Plums	June to September	Rich red-to-purple color; a firm-softness; fruity aroma	2 to 3 depending on size
Pumpkins	August to December	Heaviness in relation to size; hard, blemish-free rind; uniform bright orange color	½ to ¾ pound; 1 pound fresh pumpkin = 1 cup mashed, cooked pumpkin
Raspberries	July to September	Uniform bright red color; no mold, no attached stem caps; no oozing berries	⅓ to ½ pint
Strawberries	July to September	Bright red color; no hard spots, no mold; no bruised berries	½ pint
Tangerines	Autumn and winter	Bright, waxy, unshriveled skin; no moldy spots, bruises or blemishes	1 medium-size
Watermelon	June to September	Symmetrical shape; fresh green, tender-looking skin—no nicks, blemishes or soft spots	A 2- to 3-inch wedge

Cantaloupe Coupe

Melon and ham team well in this individual salad

Makes 6 servings

- 3 small firm ripe cantaloupes
- 3 cups cooked rice (¾ cup uncooked)
- ½ cup sliced celery
- ½ cup chopped pecans
- ½ cup golden raisins
- ½ cup mayonnaise or salad dressing
- 2 tablespoons honey
- 1 tablespoon lime juice
- ¼ teaspoon ground ginger
  Bibb or Boston lettuce
- 6 slices boiled ham (from 2 six-ounce packages)

1 Cut each cantaloupe in half crosswise; scoop out seeds, then make even sawtooth cuts around edge of each. Turn halves upside down on paper toweling to drain; cover; chill.
2 Pare cantaloupe trimmings; dice and combine with rice, celery, pecans and raisins in a large bowl.
3 Blend mayonnaise or salad dressing, honey, lime juice and ginger in a 1-cup measure; pour over rice mixture; toss lightly to mix. Chill at least an hour to season and blend flavors.
4 When ready to serve, run a knife around inside of rind of each melon half to loosen meat, then cut meat into wedges, leaving in place in shell. Place halves on serving plates.
5 Line each with 2 or 3 lettuce leaves; pile rice mixture on top. Cut each ham slice lengthwise into 4 strips; roll each into a rosette; tuck 4 into rice salad in each cantaloupe.

When you have time and your company is special, create a fantastic **Cantaloupe Coupe**.

Persimmon Salad

This exotic holidaytime delicacy combines so invitingly with avocado and greens in a lemony dressing

Makes 8 servings

- 8 cups broken mixed salad greens
- 1 firm ripe avocado, halved, peeled, seeded and sliced
- 1 persimmon, stemmed, halved and sliced
  HONEY DRESSING (recipe follows)

1 Place greens in a large salad bowl. Arrange avocado and persimmon slices, alternately, in a ring on top. (Tip: Peel avocado just before serving so it will keep its bright green color.)
2 Drizzle HONEY DRESSING over salad; toss to mix well.
HONEY DRESSING—Combine ¼ cup olive or vegetable oil, 2 tablespoons lemon juice, 1 tablespoon honey and ¼ teaspoon salt in a jar with a tight-fitting lid; shake well to mix. Makes about ½ cup.

Pagoda Fruits

What a glamorous salad, yet the arrangement is really very simple

Makes 4 servings

- 1 can (8 ounces) pear halves
- 1 can (8 ounces) cling-peach slices
- 1 can (8 ounces) figs
- 1 can (8 ounces) Royal Anne cherries
- 1 jar (5 ounces) blue-cheese spread, well chilled
  Bibb lettuce
- ½ cup mayonnaise or salad dressing
- ¼ cup honey
- 2 teaspoons syrup from fruits

1 Drain fruits; shape cheese spread into small balls. Chill all.
2 Line a serving plate with lettuce, building up center slightly. Place 4 pear halves around center; fill pear hollows with cheese balls.

Thread each of 4 kebab sticks with 2 peach slices, a fig and a cherry; stick into pears. Place remaining fruits around edge.
3 Blend remaining ingredients in a small bowl; serve separately.

Double Grapefruit Cup

Sparkly-cool and deliciously tart. Frozen fruit speeds the setting

Makes 6 servings

1 package (3 ounces) pineapple-flavor gelatin
¾ cup hot water
1 can (about 14 ounces) frozen grapefruit sections
¾ cup cold water

1 Dissolve gelatin in hot water in a medium-size bowl; add frozen grapefruit, separating pieces of fruit with a fork; stir in cold water.
2 Chill at least 25 minutes, or until softly set.
3 Spoon into glasses or small cups. Garnish with fresh mint, if you wish.

Avocado Appetizers

Perfect for a starter course. Nippy mint dressing seasons the fruit-salad filling

Makes 6 servings

1 can (11 ounces) mandarin-orange segments, drained
1 large red apple, quartered, cored and diced
1 large firm ripe banana, peeled and sliced
¼ cup vegetable oil
3 tablespoons lemon juice
1 tablespoon sugar
1 teaspoon chopped fresh mint
¼ teaspoon salt
3 medium-size firm ripe avocados

1 Set aside 12 of the mandarin-orange segments for garnish. Combine remaining with diced apple and banana in a medium-size bowl.
2 Combine vegetable oil, lemon juice, sugar, mint and salt in a small jar with a tight-fitting lid; shake well to mix. Pour 2 tablespoons over fruits; toss lightly to mix.
3 Halve avocados lengthwise, and pit but do not peel; trim a thin slice from rounded side of each, if needed, to make it set flat; place on serving plates.

Sometimes an appetizer can double as a salad. **Avocado Appetizers** is a good example.

4 Brush hollow of each with part of the remaining dressing; fill with fruit mixture. Thread saved mandarin-orange segments onto wooden picks and stick, kebab style, into salads; garnish with mint sprigs, if you wish. Serve with remaining dressing.

Gold Coast Fruit Salad

The popular fruit-and-cheese combination goes to the table salad style

Makes 8 servings

1 small fresh pineapple
2 cups (1 pint) strawberries
1 can (1 pound, 13 ounces) pear halves
4 medium-size seedless oranges
1 package (6 ounces) process Gruyere cheese
⅓ cup vegetable oil
3 tablespoons lime juice
2 tablespoons light corn syrup
½ teaspoon grated lime peel
¼ teaspoon salt
1 medium-size head Boston lettuce

1 Pare pineapple; quarter lengthwise; core. Cut fruit into bite-size pieces. Wash strawberries,

(continued)

56 • FRUIT SALAD SPECTACULARS

hull and halve. Drain syrup from pears; slice pears. Pare oranges and section. Cube cheese.
2 Combine vegetable oil, lime juice, corn syrup, lime peel and salt in a jar with a tight-fitting lid; shake well to mix.
3 Line a large salad bowl with lettuce leaves; break remainder into bite-size pieces in center of bowl. Arrange fruits in separate sections around edge on lettuce; pile cheese in center. Pour dressing over all; toss lightly to mix.

Spring Salad Bowl

Tangy pineapple and mellow avocado with greens make this refreshing salad

Makes 8 servings

- 2 cans (8¼ ounces each) pineapple chunks
- 1 large firm ripe avocado
- 8 cups broken salad greens
- ¼ cup vegetable oil
- 2 tablespoons cider vinegar
- ½ teaspoon salt
- ½ teaspoon paprika
- ¼ teaspoon ground ginger

1 Drain syrup from pineapple into a cup and set aside for Step 3. Halve avocado; remove pit and peel, then cut into thin slices.
2 Place greens in a large salad bowl; arrange avocado slices in a ring on top; mound pineapple chunks in center.
3 Combine 2 tablespoonfuls of the saved pineapple syrup with remaining ingredients in a jar with a tight-fitting lid; shake well to mix. Drizzle over salad; toss lightly to mix.

Frosted Pineapple Royale

This golden fruit makes such a pretty server, and here it's heaped with cubes of frozen fruit salad

Makes 6 servings

- 1 package (8 ounces) cream cheese, softened
- ½ cup mayonnaise or salad dressing
- 2 tablespoons 10X (confectioners' powdered) sugar
- 1 tablespoon lime juice
- 1 cup tiny marshmallows
- 1 cup orange sections
- 1 cup fresh peach slices
- ½ cup halved green grapes
- ½ cup chopped toasted slivered almonds (from a 5-ounce can)
- ¼ cup sliced maraschino cherries
- 1 cup cream for whipping
- 3 small ripe pineapples

1 Beat cream cheese with mayonnaise or salad dressing, 10X sugar and lime juice until smooth in a large bowl; stir in marshmallows, orange sections, peach slices, grapes, almonds and cherries.
2 Beat cream until stiff in a medium-size bowl; fold into cheese-fruit mixture. Pour into a shallow dish, 8x8x2; cover. Freeze several hours, or until firm.
3 Halve each pineapple lengthwise, cutting through leafy crown; cut out core, then cut fruit from rind of each half in one piece; lift out.
4 Slice enough of the fruit crosswise to make 42 thin strips; stand 7, overlapping, in each shell; chill. (Save any remaining fruit to dice and add to fruit cup for another meal.)
5 Remove fruit salad from freezer 15 minutes before serving and let stand at room temperature to soften, then cut into 1-inch cubes. Pile into pineapple shells.

Fruit-Peel Sparkles

Ginger gives this confection a subtle spicy flavor. Gelatin in the coating keeps it soft and moist. Serve, too, as candy
Makes 1½ pounds

- Peel from 3 seedless oranges
- Peel from 1 grapefruit
- 2½ cups sugar
- 1 tablespoon light corn syrup
- 1 teaspoon ground ginger
- ⅛ teaspoon salt
- 1½ cups water
- 1 teaspoon unflavored gelatin (from 1 envelope)

1 Cut orange and grapefruit peels into ⅛-inch-thick strips with scissors.
2 Place in large saucepan with water to cover. Heat to boiling; simmer 15 minutes; drain. Repeat cooking with fresh water, then draining, two more times. Return peels to saucepan.
3 Stir in 2 cups sugar, corn syrup, ginger, salt and 1 cup water. (Save remaining ½ cup sugar for Step 6 and ½ cup water for Step 5.)

FRUIT SALAD SPECTACULARS

4 Heat slowly, stirring often, to boiling, then simmer, stirring often from bottom of pan, 40 minutes, or until most of syrup is absorbed; remove from heat. (Do not overcook, as syrup will caramelize and turn brown.)
5 Soften gelatin in saved ½ cup water in 1-cup measure; stir into hot peel mixture, stirring until gelatin dissolves. Let stand until cold.
6 Lift out strips, 1 at a time; roll in saved ½ cup sugar in pie plate to coat well. Place in single layer on wax paper-lined tray or cookie sheet to set.
7 Store in a container with tight-fitting cover. This peel keeps fragrant and moist for weeks.

Papaya Coupe

The name is tropical and so is the flavor

Makes 4 servings

2 firm ripe papayas
  Lettuce
1 cup blueberries
1 cup seedless green grapes, halved
1 lime, cut in 4 wedges

1 Halve papayas; scoop out seeds; place on lettuce-lined salad plates.
2 Fill hollows with blueberries and grapes. Garnish each with a whole strawberry, if you wish, and serve with lime wedges to squeeze over.

Frozen Fruit Salad

Cooling and refreshing—serve as dessert or salad

Makes 6 servings

2 ripe bananas
1 can (6 ounces) pineapple juice
2 tablespoons lemon juice
1 cup orange juice
½ cup mayonnaise or salad dressing
1 can (11 ounces) mandarin oranges
¼ cup sugar
  Iceberg lettuce

1 Combine bananas, pineapple juice and lemon juice in electric-blender container; whirl 1 minute at low speed until smooth.
2 Add orange juice, mayonnaise or salad dressing, mandarin oranges (undrained) and sugar; whirl ½ minute at low speed.
3 Pour into 6 six-ounce molds, or into a 9x9x2-inch pan. Freeze about 4 hours, or until firm.
4 To unmold: Loosen at top edge with a sharp knife, then dip *very quickly* in and out of a pan of hot water; cover mold with serving plate; turn upside down; gently lift off mold. If molded in pan, cut into squares. Serve with lettuce and with additional mayonnaise or salad dressing, if you wish.

A salad that can serve equally as well as an appetizer, **Papaya Coupe** looks as inviting as it tastes.

Polynesian Rice Salad

This is a filling salad that can be substituted as a main dish

Makes 6 servings

- 1 cup uncooked regular rice
- ¼ pound mushrooms
- ½ cup vegetable oil
- ¼ cup cider vinegar
- 2 tablespoons soy sauce
- ½ teaspoon salt
- 1 can (11 ounces) mandarin-orange segments, drained
- 1 cup thinly sliced celery
- 1 can (5 ounces) water chestnuts, drained and sliced
- 2 tablespoons thinly sliced green onions
- Iceberg lettuce

1 Cook rice, following label directions; spoon into a large bowl.
2 While rice cooks, trim mushrooms, wash and dry well; slice lengthwise. Add to rice.
3 Combine vegetable oil, vinegar, soy sauce and salt in a jar with a tight lid; shake well to mix. Pour over rice mixture; toss lightly to mix; cover. Chill at least an hour to season.
4 Just before serving, fold in mandarin-orange segments, celery, water chestnuts and green onions. Spoon into a lettuce-lined bowl.

Tangerine Salad Bowl

With a tart flavor, this salad teams well with a tart main dish

Makes 6 servings

- 3 medium-size tangerines, peeled and sectioned
- 1 small onion, peeled, sliced, and separated into rings
- ¼ cup bottled thin French dressing
- 2 tablespoons honey
- 6 cups broken mixed salad greens
- 3 pitted ripe olives, slivered

1 Place tangerine sections and onion in separate small bowls. Drizzle each with French dressing and honey; toss lightly to mix. Chill.
2 When ready to serve, place greens in a large salad bowl. Arrange tangerine sections in a rosette on top; place onion rings around edge; pile olive slivers in center. Drizzle with any remaining dressing in bowls.

Pineapple Crown Salad

A hollowed-out pineapple is filled with fruit-goodness

Makes 8 servings

- 1 large pineapple
- 2 cups (1 pint) strawberries
- 2 medium-size seedless oranges
- 1 small firm ripe avocado
- ½ cup dairy sour cream
- ½ cup mayonnaise or salad dressing
- ¼ cup 10X (confectioners' powdered) sugar

1 Cut a slice, ¾ inch thick, from crown and bottom of pineapple; stand pineapple upright. Holding a sharp, long-blade knife vertically, insert into pineapple about ½ inch in from rind, then cut all around fruit to loosen from shell; push out fruit. Quarter lengthwise; slice core from each piece; cut fruit into bite-size pieces. Place in a large bowl.
2 Wash strawberries; hull and halve. Pare one of the oranges and section. Peel avocado; halve, pit and slice. Toss all with pineapple. Chill.
3 Grate 1 teaspoon peel from remaining orange, then squeeze 2 tablespoons juice; blend both with sour cream, mayonnaise or salad dressing, and 10X sugar in a small bowl.
4 Stand pineapple shell on a large serving plate; spoon fruit mixture into shell. Serve dressing separately.

Orange-Avocado Salad Bowl

A simple salad packed with good taste

Makes 6 servings

- 1 head Boston or leaf lettuce
- 2 oranges, peeled and sectioned
- 1 avocado, peeled, halved and diced
- Bottled oil-and-vinegar salad dressing

1 Cut core out of lettuce; separate, wash and dry leaves. Break large ones into bite-size pieces; leave small ones whole; place in a salad bowl.
2 Arrange a ring of orange sections on top; fill center with diced avocado.
3 Just before serving, toss with enough salad dressing to coat greens well.

FRUIT SALAD SPECTACULARS • 59

A main-dish salad piled high with ham and cheese strips, **Chefette Fruit Plates** will have them asking for more.

Chefette Fruit Plates

Ham and cheese strips plus a perky stuffed egg top a base of avocado, tomato, and papaya slices

Makes 6 servings

1 head iceberg lettuce, shredded fine
3 medium-size avocados, halved lengthwise, peeled, seeded and sliced
3 medium-size tomatoes, cut in wedges
2 medium-size papayas, cut in 6 one-inch-thick rings, then pared and seeded
½ pound sliced cooked ham, cut in thin strips
1 package (8 ounces) sliced Cheddar cheese, cut in thin strips
STUFFED SALAD EGGS (recipe follows)
PINEAPPLE DRESSING (recipe follows)

1 Mound lettuce, dividing evenly, onto six individual serving plates; alternate avocado and tomato slices in a ring around edge.
2 Top with a papaya slice, then strips of ham and cheese. Garnish with a STUFFED SALAD EGG. Serve with PINEAPPLE DRESSING.
  STUFFED SALAD EGGS—Hard-cook 3 eggs; shell, then halve lengthwise. Scoop out yolks and mash in a small bowl. Blend in 1 tablespoon mayonnaise or salad dressing, ½ teaspoon prepared mustard and salt and pepper to taste. Pile back into whites. Garnish with parsley. Chill until serving time. Makes 6 servings.
  PINEAPPLE DRESSING—Blend ½ cup bottled coleslaw dressing, ¼ cup drained crushed pineapple (from an 8¼ ounce can) and 2 tablespoons lemon juice in a small bowl; chill. Makes about ¾ cup.

Sunburst Salad

Avocado and cantalopue team in this slightly-sweet salad

Makes 8 servings

1 quarter wedge watermelon
1 small head romaine, washed, dried and separated into leaves
1 small cantaloupe
1 large firm ripe avocado
LEMON DRESSING (recipe follows)

1 Cut enough balls from watermelon with a melon-ball cutter or ¼ teaspoon of a measuring-spoon set to make 2 cups. (Set any remaining watermelon aside to dice and add to fruit cup for another day.)
2 Line a large round serving plate with some

(continued)

FRUIT SALAD SPECTACULARS

of the romaine leaves; break remaining into bite-size pieces and place in center.

3 Halve cantaloupe; scoop out seeds; cut cantaloupe into 8 wedges and pare. Halve avocado, pit, peel and cut into 8 wedges. Arrange cantaloupe and avocado wedges, alternately, in a ring around edge of plate; pile watermelon balls in center. Serve with LEMON DRESSING to drizzle over.

LEMON DRESSING—Combine ¼ cup olive oil or vegetable oil, 3 tablespoons lemon juice, 1 tablespoon honey and a dash of salt in a small jar with a tight-fitting cover; shake well to mix. Chill until serving time. Makes ½ cup.

Plum Compote

A salad for those who like liqueur with their meals

Makes 6 servings

¾ cup granulated sugar
1 cup water
3 one-inch pieces stick cinnamon
18 large plums, quartered and pitted
1 teaspoon grated orange peel
3 seedless oranges, pared and sectioned
¼ cup Grand Marnier liqueur
½ cup flaked coconut

Plums, oranges, flaked coconut, and liqueur team for **Plum Compote.**

FRUIT SALAD SPECTACULARS   • 61

1 Combine sugar, water and cinnamon in a large frying pan; heat to boiling. Add plums; simmer 2 minutes, or until plums are tender but still firm enough to hold their shape. Cool; remove cinnamon sticks.
2 Fold in orange peel and sections and Grand Marnier; spoon into a shallow serving bowl. Chill at least an hour.
3 Just before serving, sprinkle with coconut. Garnish with a whole plum cut into a flower shape, if you wish.

Blue Cheese Pears

Another switch on fruit and cheese. Stuff pear halves with a nippy filling, put the halves together and coat with walnuts

Makes 6 servings.

- 1/3 cup dry cottage cheese or pot cheese
- 3 or 4 ounces cream cheese
- 1/4 cup mayonnaise or salad dressing
- 3 tablespoons crumbled blue cheese
- 1 tablespoon grated lemon rind
  Red food coloring
- 2 cans (1 pound each) pear halves
- 1 cup finely chopped walnuts
  Boston lettuce

1 Press cottage cheese through a sieve into a medium-size bowl; beat in cream cheese, mayonnaise or salad dressing, blue cheese and lemon rind. Tint pale pink with food coloring. Chill in the refrigerator at least an hour to season the flavors.
2 Drain syrup from pears into a small bowl; chill to sweeten a fruit beverage.
3 Spoon 1 tablespoon of the cheese mixture into hollow of each of 6 pear halves; top each with a plain pear half. Roll in chopped walnuts on wax paper to coat all over.
4 Line 6 salad plates with lettuce; place a stuffed pear on each; spoon a dollop of remaining cheese mixture on top.

Pineapple-Cucumber Salad

Tangy fruit, cucumber and cream cheese blend into a refreshing topper for lettuce wedges

Makes 6 servings.

- 3 or 4 ounces cream cheese
- 1 can (about 8 ounces) crushed pineapple, drained
- 1/2 cup finely chopped pared cucumber
- 1/4 teaspoon salt
- 1 medium-size head iceberg lettuce

1 Soften cream cheese in a medium-size bowl; stir in drained pineapple, cucumber and salt. (If made ahead, chill until serving time, then remove from refrigerator about 1/2 hour before serving.)
2 Cut lettuce into 6 wedges; place on salad plates. Spoon cheese mixture over.

Orange-Pear Rosette

Cheese filling doubles as dressing in this two-fruit salad-dessert

Makes 4 servings at 94 calories each.

- 1 1/3 ounces Camembert cheese
- 2 tablespoons cream-style cottage cheese
- 2 medium-size fresh ripe pears
- 1 can (about 11 ounces) diet-pack mandarin-orange segments, drained
  Grated orange rind

1 Mash Camembert cheese in a small bowl; blend in cottage cheese; chill.
2 Just before serving, halve pears lengthwise and core.
3 Place a half on each of four serving plates; spoon cheese mixture into hollows. Arrange six mandarin-orange segments, petal fashion, around cheese in each; sprinkle with grated orange rind. (Save any remaining mandarin-orange segments for another day.) Weight-watcher's serving: One pear half, 6 mandarin-orange segments and 1 rounded teaspoonful cheese mixture.

Fruit Salad Palermo

The macaroni lends this salad its Italian name

Makes 8 servings

- 1 1/2 cups uncooked ditalini macaroni or elbow macaroni
- 1 small ripe banana
- 1/2 cup mayonnaise or salad dressing
- 1 tablespoon lemon juice
- 1 tablespoon honey
- 2 cups (1 pint) strawberries
- 3 medium-size seedless oranges
- 2 cups halved seedless green grapes

(continued)

FRUIT SALAD SPECTACULARS

1 Cook ditalini or elbow macaroni in boiling salted water, following label directions; drain. Place in a large bowl; cool.
2 Mash banana in a small bowl; beat in mayonnaise or salad dressing, lemon juice and honey. Pour over macaroni; toss lightly to mix. Chill.
3 Just before serving, wash strawberries; hull and slice crosswise. Pare oranges and section. Arrange strawberries, orange sections and grape halves in rows on top of macaroni mixture; garnish edge of bowl with small romaine leaves, if you wish.

Honey Pear Salad

Simplicity is the keynote to this delightful side-dish salad

Makes 6 servings

- 3 large pears, pared, cored, and diced
- 1½ cups chopped celery
- ¼ cup seedless raisins
- 3 tablespoons vegetable oil
- 2 tablespoons honey
- 2 tablespoons lemon juice
- ¼ teaspoon salt

1 Combine pears, celery, and raisins in a medium-size bowl.
2 Blend remaining ingredients in a cup; drizzle over pear mixture; toss to mix well.

Confetti Waldorf Salad

Everything's cut up like a relish—the kind of crunchy salad you eat and eat

Makes 2 servings

- 2 medium-size pared raw carrots, grated (about 1 cup)
- 1 medium-size apple, diced (about ¾ cup)
- ½ cup thinly sliced celery
- ¼ cup sliced radishes
- ¼ cup coarsely chopped pecans
- 2 tablespoons mayonnaise or salad dressing
- 1 teaspoon sugar
- ¼ teaspoon salt
- 1½ teaspoons light cream or table cream
- 1 teaspoon lemon juice

1 Combine carrot, apple, celery, radishes, and pecans in medium-size bowl.
2 Blend remaining ingredients in 1-cup measure; pour over carrot mixture, tossing to mix well. Spoon into serving bowl.

Cottage Apple Salad

The tart creamy dressing adds new flavor to a favorite fruit salad

Makes 6 servings

- 4 medium-size apples, quartered, cored and diced
- ½ cup golden raisins
- ½ cup chopped walnuts
- 1 tablespoon sugar
- 1 tablespoon lemon juice
- ¼ cup cream-style cottage cheese
- ¼ cup dairy sour cream

1 Combine apples, raisins and walnuts in medium-size bowl; sprinkle sugar and lemon juice over; toss lightly.
2 Blend cottage cheese and sour cream in 1-cup measure; spoon over apple mixture; toss lightly to mix.

Fruit Sampler

It's a sunny roundup of fruits topped with a mellow cheese-rich dressing

Makes 4 servings.

- 1 small head of leaf lettuce
- 2 oranges, peeled and sliced crosswise
- 2 pears, pared and sliced
- 2 nectarines, sliced
- 2 sweet yellow plums, halved and pitted
- ½ cup boysenberries or raspberries
- 2 tablespoons sugar
- ⅛ teaspoon ground ginger
- CAMEMBERT CREAM (recipe follows)

1 Line 4 salad plates with lettuce.
2 Arrange orange, pear and nectarine slices in

FRUIT SALAD SPECTACULARS • 63

separate mounds around edge of each plate, dividing evenly. Place a plum half in middle, hollow side up; mound berries on top.
3 Mix sugar and ginger in a small cup; sprinkle over fruits; chill. Serve with CAMEMBERT CREAM.

CAMEMBERT CREAM—Mash 2⅔ ounces Camembert cheese with fork in small bowl; slowly blend in ¼ cup heavy cream. Makes ¾ cup.

Apple Salad Cups

Plenty of different fruits give these fruit cups a robust flavor

Makes 6 servings

- 6 medium-size red eating apples
    Lemon juice
- 3 medium-size firm ripe peaches
- ½ cup thinly sliced celery
- ½ cup halved red grapes, seeded
- ½ cup tiny marshmallows
- ¼ cup coarsely broken walnuts
- ¼ cup mayonnaise or salad dressing
- ¼ cup dairy sour cream
- 1 teaspoon sugar
- ¼ teaspoon salt
    Chicory or curly endive

1 Cut a ¼-inch-thick slice from stem end of each apple; set aside. Core apples not quite to bottom, then hollow out insides, leaving shells ¼ inch thick. Make deep even sawtooth cuts into apple shells all the way around; lift out cut sections. Brush cut surfaces of apples lightly with lemon juice to prevent darkening.
2 Dice enough of the unpared apple cutouts to make 4-cups; place in a medium-size bowl. (Use all remaining apple pieces to make applesauce.)
3 Peel one of the peaches, pit and dice; add to diced apples with celery, grapes, marshmallows and walnuts.
4 Blend mayonnaise or salad dressing, sour cream, 1 teaspoon lemon juice, sugar and salt in a small bowl. Pour over apple mixture; toss lightly to mix.
5 Place each apple cup on a chicory-lined salad plate; spoon salad mixture into centers.
6 Peel remaining two peaches; pit and slice. Arrange slices around base of each salad.

When you are in the middle of a heat wave and you know the next day will be hot, prepare ahead this delectable **Salad Nicoise.**

Rainbow of Seafood Salads

Seafood and fish go well with salads. Dropped onto a bed of lettuce or folded into a molded salad, seafood and fish lend a distinctive air to any dish. You can give your meals that special appeal with one or several of the side-dish and main-dish seafood salads in these pages.

Salad Niçoise

A refreshingly simple salad that may be prepared earlier in the day, then assembled and served

Makes 6 servings

- 5 medium-size potatoes, cooked, drained and cooled
- ½ pound fresh green beans, cooked, drained and cooled
- ⅔ cup vegetable oil or olive oil
- ⅓ cup wine vinegar
- 2 cloves garlic, crushed
- 1 tablespoon prepared mustard
- 1 tablespoon chopped parsley
- ½ teaspoon instant minced onion
- 1 teaspoon salt
- ¼ teaspoon ground pepper
- 2 large tomatoes, cut into slices
- 1 red onion, cubed
- 1 small green pepper, seeded and cubed
- 6 ripe olives, halved
- 3 hard-cooked eggs, shelled and sliced
- 1 can (2 ounces) anchovy fillets, drained
- 2 medium-size heads of romaine
- 1 can (14 ounces) tuna, drained

1 Peel potatoes and cut into thick slices. Place in a shallow dish. Place beans in a second shallow dish.
2 Combine oil, vinegar, garlic, mustard, parsley, onion, salt and pepper in a jar with a tight-fitting lid; shake well to mix. Drizzle ½ cup over potatoes and 2 tablespoonfuls over beans; let each stand at least 30 minutes to season.
3 Layer vegetables, eggs, anchovies and romaine in a large salad bowl. Break tuna into chunks; arrange on top. Pour rest of dressing over; toss lightly.

Shrimp Louis Salad

Creamy make-ahead dressing and a few basic salad ingredients bring about some spectacular results

Makes about 1⅓ cups dressing, or enough for 8 servings of salad.

- 1 cup cream-style cottage cheese
- 1 hard-cooked egg, peeled and halved
- ¼ cup tomato juice
- 1 teaspoon prepared mustard
- 1 pound shrimp, cooked, peeled and deveined
- 1 avocado, peeled and sliced
- 1 cucumber, sliced
- 2 ripe olives, halved
  Assorted salad greens (we used about ½ head chicory and romaine)

1 Combine cottage cheese, egg, tomato juice and mustard in container of electric blender; whirl until smooth. Cover; chill until serving time.
2 Combine shrimp, avocado, cucumber, olives and greens in large salad bowl; toss gently. Pour chilled dressing over and toss again until well mixed. Garnish with lemon wedges, if you wish.

Shrimps Hawaiian

Sweet shrimps contrast pleasingly with tangy pineapple in a creamy dressing

Makes 6 servings.

- 2 cans (about 5 ounces each) deveined shrimps
- 1 can (about 14 ounces) pineapple chunks
- 1 can (5 ounces) water chestnuts
- 6 cups broken salad greens
- ½ cup mayonnaise or salad dressing
- ¼ cup crumbled blue cheese (about 1 ounce)

1 Drain shrimps. Drain syrup from pineapple chunks into a cup and reserve syrup for Step 3. Drain water chestnuts, then chop coarsely.
2 Place salad greens in a large bowl; pile

(continued)

shrimps, pineapple and water chestnuts in rows on top.
3 Blend 2 tablespoons of the saved pineapple syrup into mayonnaise or salad dressing and blue cheese in a small bowl; drizzle over salad; toss.

Aloha Rice-Bowl Salad with Marinated Shrimps

Plan this spectacular salad for your next summer party. It's a hostess' joy, for everything in it is a make-ahead

Makes 6 servings

1 cup uncooked regular rice
1 tablespoon vegetable oil or olive oil
1 teaspoon cider vinegar
1 teaspoon soy sauce
2 cans (8¼ ounces each) pineapple chunks
1 cup celery, sliced diagonally
¼ cup chopped green onions
½ cup mayonnaise
    MARINATED SHRIMPS (recipe follows)
    Lettuce

1 Cook rice, following label directions; if needed, drain, and place colander over hot water for 2 to 3 minutes to dry and fluff up rice kernels.
2 Mix vegetable oil or olive oil, vinegar and soy sauce in 6-cup bowl (salad will be molded in it); stir in rice and toss lightly.
3 Drain thawed pineapple chunks (save syrup for next step); stir pineapple, celery and green onions into rice mixture.
4 Blend mayonnaise with 2 tablespoons pineapple syrup from Step 3; stir into rice mixture; pat down lightly; chill at least 30 minutes.
5 Unmold onto serving platter; top with 3 MARINATED SHRIMPS; serve remaining shrimps with lettuce.

Marinated Shrimps

They're delicately sweet and tender when cooked quickly in gently bubbling seasoned water

Makes 6 servings

1½ pounds large raw shrimps in shells (16 to 24 to each pound)
  4 cups water
1 small onion, sliced
2 lemon slices
    Handful of celery tops
1 sprig parsley
1 teaspoon salt
6 peppercorns
2 whole cloves
1 bay leaf
2 tablespoons vegetable oil
2 tablespoons lemon juice

1 Wash shrimps in colander under running cold water; shell by splitting feelers open and turning shell back, then easing shrimp out with force of water; make a shallow cut down back of each; remove black line, or sand vein, with tip of knife; make cut a bit deeper so shrimps will curl up when cooked.
2 Heat water, onion, lemon, celery tops, parsley, salt, peppercorns, cloves and bay leaf to boiling in large frying pan, then simmer 2 to 3 minutes.
3 Drop in prepared shrimps; heat just to boiling, then simmer 3 to 5 minutes, or until shrimps are pink (do not let water boil; it will overcook and toughen them).
4 Remove with slotted spoon to a medium-size bowl; sprinkle with mixture of vegetable oil and lemon juice; cover; chill until serving time.

Bayou Shrimp Salad

This is a full-bodied salad for those who like Creole cookery

Makes 8 to 10 servings

1 cup uncooked regular rice
1 teaspoon sugar
½ teaspoon grated lime peel
2 tablespoons lime juice
1½ cups diced cooked ham (½ pound)
1 cup sliced celery
½ cup diced green pepper
1 package (12 ounces) frozen deveined shelled raw shrimps
1 package (10 ounces) frozen whole okra
6 tablespoons bottled thin French dressing
½ cup mayonnaise or salad dressing
1 tablespoon chopped parsley
1 cup halved cherry tomatoes
    Salt and pepper
    Romaine

1 Cook rice, following label directions; drain well. Place in a large bowl; stir in sugar, lime peel and juice, ham, celery and green pepper.

RAINBOW OF SEAFOOD SALADS • 67

2 Cook shrimps and okra in separate medium-size saucepans, following label directions; drain well.
3 Dice remaining shrimps, but leave okra whole; add shrimps and okra to rice-ham mixture; drizzle French dressing over; toss to mix. Chill at least 30 minutes to season and blend flavors.
4 Just before serving, fold in mayonnaise or salad dressing, parsley and cherry tomatoes. Season to taste with salt and pepper.

Shrimp and Lobster Salad in Artichoke Petal Cups

This is not an easy salad to put together, but the result is worth all the effort

Makes 4 servings

    4 small fresh artichokes
      Boiling salted water
      Olive oil
    1 can (about 6 ounces) flaked lobster, drained
    1 can (about 5 ounces) deveined shrimps, drained
  ½ cup diced celery
  ¼ cup dairy sour cream
    1 tablespoon chili sauce
    1 tablespoon lemon juice
      Lemon wedges

1 Snip tops and prickly leaf tips and remove stem bottoms from artichokes; cook, covered, in boiling salted water seasoned with a few drops olive oil 30 to 45 minutes or until tender. Drain; let stand until cool enough to handle; separate leaves enough to cut out "choke" at base; chill.
2 Mix together all remaining ingredients except lemon wedges and chill well.
3 To serve, spoon shrimp and lobster mixture into artichoke petal cups and garnish with lemon wedges.

Serve **Shrimp and Lobster in Artichoke Petal Cups** at a luncheon or let it star on a buffet.

Any chef's salad is a joy to see and to eat. **Seafood Chef's Salad** will have your guests dipping into the bowl several times.

Seaside Macaroni Salad

Pack it in ice—add the limas and celery just before serving

Makes 6 servings

- ½ cup uncooked elbow macaroni
- 1 package (1 pound) frozen deveined shelled shrimps
- ½ cup bottled French dressing
- 1 package (10 ounces) frozen baby lima beans, cooked, drained and chilled
- ½ cup finely chopped celery
- ½ cup mayonnaise or salad dressing
- 2 tablespoons finely chopped parsley
  Boston lettuce
- 2 small tomatoes, cut in very thin wedges

1 Cook macaroni, following label directions; drain; place in a large bowl.
2 Cook shrimp, following label directions; drain; add to macaroni. Drizzle French dressing over top; toss lightly to mix. Chill at least an hour to season.
3 Just before serving, add limas and celery to macaroni mixture; fold in mayonnaise or salad dressing. Spoon into a lettuce-lined bowl; place tomato wedges around edge in bowl.

Seafood Chef's Salad

Chill just so that the softness is gone from the seafood

Makes 4 servings

- 1 head Boston or leaf lettuce
- 1 can (7 ounces) king crabmeat
- 2 hard-cooked eggs, shelled
- 10 radishes

MARINATED SCALLOPS (recipe follows)
CARROT CURLS (recipe follows)
1 cup (8 ounce container) cottage cheese
Paprika
TOMATO DRESSING (recipe follows)

1 Line a large salad bowl with lettuce leaves; break up remaining lettuce into bite-size pieces into bowl.
2 Drain and pick over crabmeat, removing any bits of bone but keeping meat in big chunks. Quarter eggs lengthwise. Wash and slice radishes.
3 Arrange in mounds with MARINATED SCALLOPS and CARROT CURLS in a ring on lettuce. Fill center with cottage cheese; dust with paprika. Serve with TOMATO DRESSING.

Marinated Scallops

Fresh or frozen, scallops look and taste good in any salad

Makes 4 servings

½ pound (about 20) sea scallops
  OR: 1 package (7 ounces) frozen sea scallops
2 cups water
1 slice of onion
1 slice of lemon
2 peppercorns
3 tablespoons TOMATO DRESSING (recipe follows)

1 Wash fresh scallops under cold running water; drain. (Keep frozen scallops in iced block.)
2 Heat water, onion, lemon and peppercorns to boiling in medium-size saucepan; simmer 5 minutes. Add scallops; cover; simmer 5 minutes (7 to 10 minutes, if frozen).
3 Remove with slotted spoon; drain well; place in shallow dish. Spoon TOMATO DRESSING over to marinate; cover; chill.

Carrot Curls

Chilly ice-water bath makes these crisp strips curl neatly.
Scrape and halve 2 carrots lengthwise. Shave into long paper-thin strips with vegetable parer. Roll each strip around finger; slide off into a bowl of ice water; let stand to curl.

Tomato Dressing

Count just 3 calories for each tablespoonful of this zippy dressing

Makes about 1¼ cups

1 envelope French-dressing mix
¾ cup tomato juice
¼ cup cider vinegar
2 tablespoons water

Combine all ingredients in 2-cup jar with screw top; shake well; chill. Shake again just before using.

Crab Louis Pielets

Each little shell holds crunchy crab salad framed with zippy-seasoned asparagus

Bake tart shells at 425° for 15 minutes.
Makes 6 servings

1 package piecrust mix
2 packages (10 ounces each) frozen asparagus spears
1 tablespoon bottled oil-and-vinegar dressing
3 cans (about 7 ounces each) crabmeat
1 can (5 ounces) water chestnuts, drained and chopped
  LOUIS DRESSING (recipe follows)
2 heads Bibb lettuce, washed and dried
1 lime, cut into 12 thin slices

1 Prepare piecrust mix, following label directions. Roll out, half at a time, ⅛ inch thick, on a lightly floured pastry cloth or board; cut each into 3 six-inch rounds, using a saucer for pattern. Fit into 4-inch tart-shell pans, pressing firmly against bottoms and sides; trim overhang to ½ inch; turn under, flush with rim; flute edge. Prick well all over with a fork.
2 Bake in hot oven (425°) 15 minutes, or until golden; cool completely in pans on a wire rack, then remove carefully.
3 Cook asparagus, following label directions; drain. Cut off head of each spear about 1½ inches down; place heads in a pie plate; drizzle with oil-and-vinegar dressing; chill. Cut remaining asparagus stalks in ½-inch-long pieces; place in a medium-size bowl.
4 Drain crabmeat; set aside a few large pieces for garnish, then flake remaining, removing bony tissue, if any. Add with water chestnuts to asparagus in bowl.

(continued)

RAINBOW OF SEAFOOD SALADS

5 Make LOUIS DRESSING; spoon 2 tablespoons over crab mixture; toss lightly to mix; chill.
6 When ready to serve, line 6 individual serving plates with lettuce. Stand asparagus spears around edges in tart shells; spoon crab mixture in centers; place on plates. Garnish each tartlet with saved pieces of crab and 2 slices of lime, twisted. Serve with remaining LOUIS DRESSING to spoon over.

LOUIS DRESSING—Blend ½ cup mayonnaise or salad dressing, ½ cup dairy sour cream, ¼ cup catsup, 3 tablespoons chopped green onion, 1 teaspoon sugar, 1 tablespoon lime juice, and a few drops liquid red pepper seasoning in a small bowl; chill. Makes about 1½ cups.

CRAB KNOW-HOW

One of our extra-special shellfish treats, it comes as choice lump meat, flake meat or lump and flake combined. Lump, highest in price, is the choice where color is important. The other two, both thriftier, are excellent for casseroles and creamed dishes or sandwich spreads. Newest comer to the market is "cold-packed" crabmeat. Here the crab is cooked, packed in vacuum tins and shipped in ice. Since it's a refrigerated canned item, most supermarkets stock it in the fish or meat departments.

Shrimp and Crab Cocktail

Chill the seafood so there is a good contrast with the sauce

Makes 8 servings

1 pound medium-size fresh shrimps
  OR: 1 package (10 or 12 ounces) frozen shrimps in shells
1 teaspoon salt
1 small onion, sliced
2 slices lemon
1 bay leaf
1 can (about 5 ounces) king crabmeat
  PEPPY GUACAMOLE SAUCE (recipe follows)

1 Wash, shell and devein shrimps.
2 Half-fill a large frying pan with water; season with salt, onion, lemon and bay leaf; heat to boiling. Add shrimps; reheat until bubbling, then simmer 4 to 5 minutes, or just until tender, (do not overcook, as this toughens them); drain; chill.
3 Drain crabmeat and cut it into bite-size pieces, removing any thin bony tissue; chill.
4 Divide seafoods among 8 sherbet glasses, saving 8 shrimps for garnish; top with PEPPY GUACAMOLE SAUCE, then shrimps.

PEPPY GUACAMOLE SAUCE—Halve, pit, peel and mash a medium-size ripe avocado in small bowl (you should have about 1 cup). Blend in ¼ cup mayonnaise, 2 tablespoons lemon juice, 1 teaspoon salt and ¼ teaspoon liquid red pepper seasoning. (If sauce is tightly covered, it will keep its rich green color for an hour before serving.) Makes 8 servings.

Louisiana Crab Salad

This is not Louisiana-Creole but Louisiana-southern

Makes 4 to 6 servings

3 cups warm cooked rice
2 tablespoons bottled Italian-style salad dressing
1 can (about 5 ounces) crabmeat, drained and flaked
1 cup finely diced celery
2 diced pimientos
2 tablespoons lemon juice
1 tablespoon chopped fresh dill
1 teaspoon grated onion
¼ teaspoon salt
¼ cup mayonnaise or salad dressing
  Salad greens

1 Marinate rice with salad dressing in medium-size bowl; let stand at room temperature about 1 hour, then chill.
2 Combine crabmeat, celery, pimientos, lemon juice, dill, onion and salt in second bowl; cover; chill.
3 To serve, combine rice and crabmeat mixture; fold in mayonnaise or salad dressing; serve on crisp salad greens; garnish with sprigs of dill, if you wish.

King Crab Salad Bowls

Take a little extra time arranging the ingredients, and the salad will disappear fast

Makes 6 servings

¾ cup mayonnaise or salad dressing
¼ cup chili sauce

2 tablespoons lemon juice
¼ cup sliced green onions
2 tablespoons finely chopped parsley
2 cans (about 8 ounces each) king crabmeat
4 slices processed white American cheese
2 firm ripe avocados
1 small head iceberg lettuce
¼ cup toasted sliced almonds

1 Blend mayonnaise or salad dressing, chili sauce, lemon juice, green onions and parsley in a small bowl; chill at least a half hour to season.
2 Pick over crabmeat, removing bony tissue, if any; flake crab. Cut cheese into julienne strips. Halve avocados; peel, pit and dice.
3 Shred lettuce; divide among 6 individual salad bowls. Place crabmeat, cheese strips and avocados in rows over lettuce; sprinkle with almonds. Pass dressing separately to spoon on top.

Seaside Success

Here's popular tuna salad with a skillet twist. Chinese noodles and shredded lettuce are the crisp extras

Makes 6 servings

1 envelope instant vegetable broth
  OR: 1 vegetable-bouillon cube
1 teaspoon instant minced onion
½ cup diced celery
½ cup water
2 cans (about 7 ounces each) tuna, drained and flaked
4 hard-cooked eggs, shelled and coarsely chopped
½ cup mayonnaise or salad dressing
¼ cup sliced stuffed green olives
1 tablespoon chopped parsley
2 teaspoons lemon juice
1 small head iceberg lettuce, washed and shredded
1 can (3 ounces) Chinese fried noodles

1 Combine vegetable broth or bouillon cube, onion, celery and water in a medium-size frying pan; cover. Heat to boiling; simmer 5 minutes.
2 Add tuna and eggs; cover. Heat just until bubbly-hot; remove from heat.
3 Blend mayonnaise or salad dressing, olives, parsley and lemon juice in a cup; spoon over tuna mixture. Toss lightly to mix; push to one side.
4 Place shredded lettuce in a pile in pan; sprinkle noodles over tuna. Serve warm right from the skillet.

Tuna Supper Salad

It's hearty with tuna, cheese and limas seasoned with spicy French dressing

Makes 6 servings.

2 cans (about 7 ounces each) tuna, drained and broken up
2 tablespoons lemon juice
¼ teaspoon seasoned pepper
1 can (1 pound) lima beans, drained
¼ cup bottled French dressing
6 cups broken salad greens
4 slices Muenster cheese, cut in strips
12 pitted ripe olives, quartered

1 Toss tuna lightly with lemon juice and seasoned pepper in a small bowl. Toss limas with French dressing in a second small bowl. Chill both to season and blend flavors.
2 Place salad greens in a large bowl; pile tuna, limas, cheese strips and olives in rows, spoke fashion, on top. Garnish with pimiento strips and cashew nuts, if you wish. Toss, salad style, at the table, adding more French dressing, if you wish.

TUNA KNOW-HOW

This favorite shares honors with salmon as tops in popularity among canned seafood items. Because the kind of fish that goes into the can and the price vary, it's good shopping practice to know what you're buying.

Two of your best guides are White Meat and Light Meat, stamped right on the label. "White meat" simply means Albacore—the whitest, fanciest and most expensive tuna—has been used. "Light meat" tuna is packed from all the other plentiful kinds of tuna that are similar in color and flavor, and is an excellent all-purpose choice.

Another factor affecting the price is grade, so look to the label again. "Solid pack" consists of large pieces of choice fish loins and, understandably, costs a little more. "Chunk" tuna, cut in small pieces, carries a moderate price tag, and for the thriftiest buy of all, your dependables are "grated" or "flaked."

Lobster Salad Supreme

Pile salad into lobster shells and garnish with the jumbo claws

Makes 4 servings

- 4 small live lobsters (about 1 pound each)
- 1 cup chopped celery
- 1 cup chopped green pepper
- ½ cup mayonnaise or salad dressing
- 1 tablespoon lime juice
- Salt and pepper
- TOMALLEY-STUFFED EGGS (recipe follows)

1 Drop live lobsters into a very large kettle of rapidly boiling salted water; cover. Keep heat high and cook 10 to 15 minutes. Lobsters will turn a bright red. Remove at once with tongs; drain until cool enough to handle. (If you do not have a very large kettle, cook lobsters, 2, or even 1, at a time, adding more water and heating to boiling each time.)
2 Remove meat from each lobster, saving shell for restuffing, this way: Place lobster on its back; twist off the 2 large claws and set aside for Step 4. Cut lobster down middle from head to tail, being careful not to cut through hard shell of back. Twist and gently pull small claws away. Cut away the thin membrane on either side of tail with kitchen scissors and lift out meat. Save the green tomalley (liver), and pink coral (roe), if any, for stuffing eggs.
3 Discard the stomach sac or "lady" in back of head, black vein running from head to tail and spongy gray tissue.
4 Set the 4 lobster shells and 8 large ends of claws from Step 2 aside. Crack rest of claw pieces; remove meat with a metal pick and place in a medium-size bowl. Dice meat from tail and add to bowl.
5 Stir in celery, green pepper, mayonnaise or salad dressing, lime juice and salt and pepper to taste. Pile back into lobster shells, dividing evenly.
6 Place on salad plates; garnish each with the 2 large claw pieces, cracked, and watercress, if you wish. Serve with TOMALLEY-STUFFED EGGS.

TOMALLEY-STUFFED EGGS—Shell 4 hard-cooked eggs and halve crosswise. Remove yolks and press through a sieve into a small bowl. Blend in saved lobster tomalley and roe and ¼ cup mayonnaise or salad dressing; pile back into whites. Garnish each with a tiny square of green pepper. Makes 4 servings.

Neptune's Tower

It's amazing how fast you can build this spectacular with ready-seasoned canned and packaged foods

Makes 8 servings

- 1 jar (1 pound) pickled green beans
- 1 can (about 1 pound) green peas with onions
- 1 can (1 pound) sliced carrots
- 1 can (about 8 ounces) salmon
- 1 can (about 7 ounces) tuna
- 1 can (about 6 ounces) lobster meat
- 1 can (5 ounces) deveined shrimps
- 1 jar (12 ounces) olive salad
- 1 head iceberg lettuce
- 2 containers (1 pound each) prepared potato salad

1 Drain liquid from beans into a cup; set beans aside for step 5. Drain peas and carrots; place in separate small bowls; drizzle each with half of the saved bean liquid; set aside for Step 3.
2 Drain salmon, tuna, and lobster; drain and rinse shrimps. Break salmon and tuna into large chunks. Set aside a few pieces of lobster meat and 1 or 2 shrimps for a garnish, then dice remaining.
3 Drain olive salad, cut up any large pieces. Drain peas and carrots.
4 Break lettuce into bite-size pieces; place in a layer on a shallow large serving platter.
5 Layer remaining foods, building up to a pyramid shape, on top of lettuce this way: Potato salad; peas; tuna, salmon, diced lobster and shrimps; olive salad; carrots; beans. Garnish with saved lobster, shrimps, watercress, and serve with mayonnaise or salad dressing, if you wish.

Cape Cod Scallop Salad

Another favorite from the sea goes high style with crisp vegetables in a creamy dressing

Makes 4 servings

- 1 pound fresh or frozen sea scallops
- 2 tablespoons butter or margarine, melted
- 2 tablespoons bottled Italian salad dressing
- 1 tablespoon chopped parsley
- ½ teaspoon grated lemon peel
- 1 cup chopped celery
- ½ cup sliced radishes
- ¼ cup thinly sliced cucumber
- ¼ cup mayonnaise or salad dressing
- 1 head of lettuce

1 Wash fresh scallops under running cold water, or partly thaw frozen ones. Cut each in thin slices.
2 Coat slices well with melted butter or margarine in a large frying pan; cover; cook slowly 5 minutes.
3 Lift out with slotted spoon and place in a medium-size bowl; toss with Italian dressing, parsley and lemon rind; cover. Chill several hours to season and blend flavors.
4 Stir in celery, radishes, cucumber and mayonnaise or salad dressing.
5 Make nests of lettuce in 4 individual salad bowls or seashells. Spoon scallop salad into centers; garnish each with a "flower" of sliced cucumber, radish and ripe olive, if you wish.

Salata

"Salata" is the Greek word for salad—and this one comes complete with the feta cheese—made here from cow's milk instead of the goat's milk used traditionally in Greece

Makes 6 servings.

- 1 small head Boston lettuce
- ¼ cup chopped green onions or scallions
- 2 medium-size potatoes, cooked, peeled and sliced (2 cups)
- 2 cups cherry tomatoes, sliced
- 2 cans (2 ounces each) flat anchovy fillets
- ¼ cup coarsely chopped parsley
- 1 bunch radishes, trimmed and sliced
- ½ cup crumbled feta cheese
- 1 cup Greek olives or 1 cup pitted ripe olives, halved
- ¼ cup olive or vegetable oil
- 2 tablespoons lemon juice
- ½ teaspoon leaf oregano, crumbled
- ½ teaspoon salt
- Freshly ground pepper

1 Line a large deep platter or shallow bowl with lettuce leaves, then break remainder into bite-size pieces and place in center; sprinkle green onions over lettuce.
2 Layer potatoes, tomatoes, anchovies, parsley, radishes and cheese on top. Place olives in a ring around base; garnish cheese with a wedge of lemon, if you wish.
3 Combine olive oil, lemon juice, oregano, salt and pepper in a jar with a tight lid; shake well to mix.
4 Just before serving, drizzle dressing over vegetable mixture; toss lightly to mix.

SALMON KNOW-HOW

What would we do without this standby? Here too you'll find a wide range of prices for the familiar 1-pound tall or ½-pound flat tins, depending on the color of the meat. Usually the highest priced salmon has the reddest color, the firmest flakes and is packed in the richest oil.

All varieties can be used interchangeably, but some are preferable for salads or cold plates because of their pretty color; others taste just as good in cooked dishes. From highest to lowest in price, they rank like this: Chinook or King; Red or Sockeye; Medium Red or Silver; Pink, Chum or Keta.

Senegalese Salmon Salad

The curry-flavor rice mix gives this salad a distinctive taste

Makes 6 servings

- 1 package (6 ounces) curry-flavor rice mix
- Butter or margarine
- Water
- 1 can (1 pound) salmon
- 1 cup diced celery
- ¼ cup sliced stuffed olives
- 2 teaspoons grated lemon peel
- ¼ cup cream for whipping
- ½ cup mayonnaise or salad dressing
- Iceberg lettuce

1 Prepare rice mix with butter or margarine and water, following label directions. Place in a large bowl; cool, then cover and chill about an hour.
2 While rice chills, drain liquid from salmon; remove skin and bones. Flake salmon; fold into rice mixture with celery, olives and lemon peel.
3 Beat cream until stiff in a small bowl; fold in mayonnaise or salad dressing; fold into salmon mixture.
4 Place lettuce leaves on serving plates to form cups; spoon salmon mixture into cups. Garnish with sliced olives.

A medley of vegetable dishes combine in this colorful display. Stuffed tomatoes, sweet potatoes that spoon into a salad, asparagus with a hollandaise sauce, and broccoli go with many main-dish and side-dish salads.

Garden Fresh Salads

It's back to nature with an abundance of salads taken from the garden. Vegetables in all colors and with different tastes group together in these mouth-watering main-dish and side-dish salads. Preferably, use only fresh vegetables. But during the long, cold winter months, don't forget frozen vegetables. Either way, you'll have vegetable salads you'll be proud to have grace any dining or picnic table.

Summer Garden Potato Salad

Most popular of all picnic salads—this one with an easy molding trick

Makes 6 servings

- 6 large potatoes, cooked, peeled and cut into small cubes
- 3 hard-cooked eggs, shelled and chopped
- ¾ cup chopped dill pickles
- ¾ cup sliced radishes
- ½ cup chopped green onions
- 1 teaspoon salt
- 1 teaspoon dillweed
- ¼ teaspoon pepper
- 1¼ cups mayonnaise or salad dressing
  Salad greens
  STUFFED-EGG DAISIES (recipe follows)
  Cherry tomatoes

1 Combine potatoes, eggs, pickles, radishes, green onions, salt, dillweed and pepper in large bowl; stir in mayonnaise or salad dressing with a spoon until thoroughly blended (mixture will be moist). Chill at least 2 hours to blend and mellow flavors.

2 When ready to put salad together, break salad greens into bite-size pieces in large salad bowl; mound potato salad into a cone on top (it will pat quickly into shape with 2 spoons). Surround cone with STUFFED-EGG DAISIES and cherry tomatoes.

Note—Cover lightly with transparent wrap or foil. Or set bowl in shallow box and pack crumpled paper around it to hold it steady. Keep cool en route in an insulated tote bag or foam chest.

Stuffed-Egg Daisies

Each perky flower-shape cup hides a tangy stuffed olive.

Hard-cook and shell 6 eggs. Holding each upright, draw a guideline around middle with tip of knife, then make even saw-tooth cuts into egg above and below the line all the way around. Carefully pull halves apart; remove yolks and mash in small bowl. Blend in 2 tablespoons mayonnaise, 1 teaspoon prepared mustard and salt and pepper to taste. Place a small stuffed green olive in each egg-white half, then fill with yolk mixture; chill. Makes 6 servings.

Dilled Potato-Salad Platter

There's plenty of taste in this easy-to-make salad

Makes 12 servings

- 5 pounds medium-size potatoes, pared
- 2 cups chopped celery
- 1 medium-size onion, chopped (½ cup)
- 2 cups mayonnaise or salad dressing
- ½ cup milk
- 2 tablespoons dill seeds, crushed
- 1 teaspoon salt
  Dash of pepper
  Boston lettuce
  STUFFED EGGS (recipe follows)
- 1 tablespoon chopped parsley

1 Cook potatoes, covered, in boiling salted water in a large saucepan 45 minutes, or just until tender; drain. Cool until easy to handle, then cube and combine with celery and onion in a large bowl.
2 Blend mayonnaise or salad dressing, milk, dill seeds, salt, and pepper in a small bowl; fold into potato mixture.
3 Spoon into a 12-cup bowl; press down lightly with back of spoon to make top even; cover. Chill several hours.
4 When ready to serve, loosen salad around edge with a thin-blade knife; invert onto a serving plate; lift off bowl. Frame salad with lettuce; arrange STUFFED EGGS around edge. Sprinkle

(continued)

salad with parsley and garnish with shredded green-onion tops, if you wish.

STUFFED EGGS—Hard-cook 12 eggs; shell. Cut each in half lengthwise; scoop out yolks into a medium-size bowl; mash well. Stir in ½ cup mayonnaise or salad dressing and 1 tablespoon prepared mustard. Pile back into whites. Top each with red caviar (from a 4-ounce jar).

Potato Cones

Perfect make-aheads for that extra-special outdoors meal

Makes 8 servings

- 6 medium-size potatoes, pared and diced
- 1½ cups dairy sour cream
- 1 envelope blue-cheese salad dressing mix
- 1 cup finely chopped celery
- 2 packages (6 ounces each) sliced ham-bologna (16 slices)
- Parsley

1 Cook potatoes, covered, in boiling salted water in a large saucepan 15 minutes, or until tender; drain. Return potatoes to pan and shake over low heat until dry and fluffy. Press through a ricer or mash in a large bowl; cool slightly.
2 Blend sour cream and blue-cheese dressing mix in a small bowl; beat into potatoes; stir in celery.
3 Curl each slice of ham-bologna into a cornucopia; fasten with a wooden pick. Spoon potato mixture into each to fill. (Or press through a pastry bag into cornucopias.) Arrange in a single layer on a large serving platter; cover. Chill at least 2 hours to season.
4 Just before serving, garnish each cornucopia with a tiny sprig of parsley; garnish platter with lettuce and radish roses, if you wish.

Double Bean Salad Bowls

For a change, make salad your first course. It's surprisingly filling, so you won't be as hungry for the rest of the meal

Makes 6 servings, 48 calories each

- 1 package (9 ounces) frozen cut green beans
- 1 package (9 ounces) frozen wax beans
- 6 tablespoons bottled low-calorie French dressing
- ½ small head iceberg lettuce

1 Cook green and wax beans in separate saucepans, following label directions; drain, Place each in a small bowl; drizzle with 3 tablespoons of the salad dressing; toss lightly to mix. Chill at least an hour to season.
2 Just before serving, shred lettuce coarsely; place in 6 individual salad bowls. Spoon beans, dividing evenly, in separate piles on top. Garnish each salad with several small white onion rings, if you wish.

HOW TO CARE FOR AND STORE GREENS:

Perfect salads start with perfect greens, and if you clean them and put them into the refrigerator fast, they should keep fresh and crisp for about a week.

Remove stems and any droopy leaves, then wash solid heads such as iceberg lettuce and cabbage and dry on paper toweling, or set on a wire rack or in a colander to drain. Swish leafy varieties such as Boston or leaf lettuce and curly endive up and down in a pan of lukewarm water, changing it, if needed. Warm water won't wilt the greens and helps to wash away every speck of soil or sand that much faster. Give greens a final rinsing in very cold water and drain well.

Store cleaned big heads in your vegetable crisper or large plastic bag, smaller varieties in individual bags.

Save the dark outer vitamin-rich leaves, unless they are badly bruised, to shred into a salad or put into sandwiches where appearance isn't so important. Store delicate greens such as mint and watercress in small covered containers.

Italian Bean Bowl

Men will go for this hearty salad with its zippy seasoned beans and chick peas, plus julienne cold cuts

Makes 4 to 6 servings

- 1 envelope Italian salad-dressing mix
- Red wine vinegar
- Olive oil
- 1 package (10 ounces) frozen Italian green beans, cooked and drained

GARDEN FRESH SALADS • 77

1 can (about 1 pound) chick peas, drained
1 medium-size red onion, chopped
1 small head of lettuce
1 package (6 ounces) Italian assortment sliced cold cuts, cut into julienne strips

1 Prepare salad-dressing mix with vinegar, olive oil, and water, following label directions.
2 Combine green beans, chick peas, and onion in a medium-size bowl; drizzle ¼ cup salad dressing over; toss lightly to mix. Let stand at least an hour to season and blend flavors. (Save remaining salad dressing for salad for another meal.)
3 When ready to serve, partly fill a salad bowl with lettuce; spoon bean mixture on top; add meat; toss lightly to mix well.

Picnic Bean Salad

White and red kidney beans go well with celery and mayonnaise in this flavorful salad

Makes 6 servings

1 jar (about 8 ounces) sweet mustard pickles
½ cup mayonnaise or salad dressing
½ teaspoon sugar
1 can (1 pound, 4 ounces) white kidney beans, drained
1 can (1 pound) red kidney beans, drained
1½ cups finely chopped celery

1 Drain dressing from pickles into a small bowl. Measure 3 tablespoonfuls and blend with mayonnaise or salad dressing and sugar in a cup.
2 Spoon white beans, red beans and celery in rings on a deep serving platter; pile pickles in center.
3 Just before serving, drizzle dressing over all; toss lightly to mix.

Chili-Bean Salad

Treat the chili powder with respect—too much, and your salad will lose its careful blending

Makes 6 servings

2 teaspoons chili powder
¼ cup olive oil or vegetable oil
2 tablespoons vinegar
2 teaspoons sugar
¼ teaspoon salt
2 cans (about 1 pound each) kidney beans, drained

1 large green pepper, diced (1 cup)
1 small Bermuda onion, diced (1 cup)
1 cup pitted ripe olives, halved
2 tablespoons catsup
1 tablespoon mayonnaise or salad dressing
1 small head of iceberg or leaf lettuce
1 package (8 ounces) sliced process American cheese

1 Heat chili powder in olive oil or vegetable oil in small saucepan about 2 minutes to develop flavor; remove from heat. Stir in vinegar, sugar, and salt; stir into drained beans in large bowl; let stand about 30 minutes to season.
2 Stir in green pepper, onion, olives, catsup, and mayonnaise or salad dressing; toss lightly to mix.
3 Shred lettuce coarsely, saving some leafy tops for garnish; place in a large salad bowl. Spoon bean mixture on top; tuck leafy tops around edge.
4 Quarter cheese slices; arrange, overlapping, in 2 circles on top of bean mixture.

Green-and-Gold Vegetable Bowl

Sunny carrots and green beans make this bright go-with for a cold-cut platter

Makes 6 servings

1 can (about 1 pound) cut green beans, drained
1 cup sliced celery
2 cans (about 1 pound each) sliced carrots, drained
¼ cup vegetable oil
2 tablespoons lemon juice
1 teaspoon instant minced onion
1 teaspoon dried parsley flakes
1 teaspoon sugar
½ teaspoon salt
Lettuce

1 Toss beans with celery in a small bowl; place carrots in a second bowl. Mix vegetable oil, lemon juice, onion, parsley flakes, sugar, and salt in a cup; drizzle half over carrots and remaining over beans; toss each lightly. Chill to season and blend flavors.
2 Spoon carrot and bean mixtures in separate piles in a lettuce-lined shallow serving bowl. Serve with mayonnaise or salad dressing, if you wish.

A GALLERY OF POPULAR SALAD GREENS

From chunky crisp iceberg lettuce to peppery watercress—here are the leaders of the salad-greens family. Use your favorite in your salad bowl, or mix them for a contrast of two is good; three, even better.

Iceberg or Head Lettuce—Big round compact head with light to dark green leaves. Everyday favorite.

Boston or Butterhead Lettuce—Soft loose head with tender delicately flavored green to light yellow leaves.

Romaine or Cos Lettuce—Long green crisp leaves with heavy ribs. Popular for mixed green-salad bowls.

Bibb or Limestone Lettuce—Tiny head of dark green leaves. Prized for its size, color, flavor, tenderness.

Leaf or Garden Lettuce—Ruffled pale green delicate leaves growing loosely from its small slender stalk.

Green Cabbage—Spring variety is bright green; late or winter, silvery green. An all-year winner for coleslaw.

Red or Purple Cabbage—Easily recognized by color. Solid heavy head with a flavor stronger than the green.

Savoy or Curly Cabbage—Tightly crimped, heavily veined dark green leaves with a green-cabbage flavor.

Chinese or Celery Cabbage—Long oval compact head of pale green to white frilly leaves. Chop for salad.

Belgian or French Endive—Tiny tight sticklike head of cream-white leaves. A European-grown specialty.

Chicory or Curly Endive—Floppy head with feathery dark to very pale green leaves. Pleasingly bitter flavor.

Escarole—Cross between lettuce and chicory with broad curly leaves and yellowish center. Slightly bitter.

Spinach—Dark green flat crinkly leaves with coarse stems. For salad, use tender leaves with stems removed.

Watercress—Little shiny dark green leaves branching out from a slender stalk. Tastes bitey, pungent.

GARDEN FRESH SALADS • 79

Sweet-Sour Brown Beans

Sugar and vinegar provide the accents in this picnic favorite

Makes 12 servings

 2 pounds dried Swedish brown beans
10 cups water
 3 teaspoons salt
½ cup firmly packed brown sugar
½ cup cider vinegar
   Sliced green onions

1 Wash beans and sort; combine with water in a kettle.
2 Heat to boiling; cook 2 minutes; cover. Remove from heat; let stand 1 hour.
3 Stir in salt and just enough water, if needed, to cover beans. Heat to boiling; simmer 1½ hours, or until beans are tender. (If needed during cooking, add additional water.)
4 Stir in brown sugar and vinegar; heat 10 minutes to blend flavors. Spoon into a heated serving bowl; sprinkle with sliced green onions.
Note—If you cannot find Swedish brown beans in your supermarket, substitute dried red kidney beans.

Mustard Bean Bowl

Garlic cuts the mustard and lends a subtle taste to this bean salad

Makes 6 servings

1 can (1 pound, 4 ounces) white kidney beans, drained
1 can (1 pound) red kidney beans, drained
1 clove of garlic, crushed
1 package (10 ounces) fresh spinach
½ cup mayonnaise or salad dressing
½ cup dairy sour cream
2 tablespoons prepared mustard
½ teaspoon seasoned salt
¼ teaspoon seasoned pepper

1 Place white and red beans in separate bowls; toss each with half of the garlic; cover. Let stand several hours to season.
2 Trim stems and any coarse leaves from spinach; wash leaves and dry well; break into bite-size pieces. Place in a large salad bowl; spoon beans in separate sections on top.
3 Blend mayonnaise or salad dressing with sour cream, mustard, salt and pepper in a small bowl; pour over bean mixture. Toss lightly to mix.

Fassoul Iahnia

To the Bulgarians this is white beans in olive oil

Makes 6 servings

2 cans (1 pound, 4 ounces each) white kidney beans, drained
½ cup chopped parsley
1 small green pepper, halved, seeded, and diced
1 small onion, chopped (¼ cup)
2 cloves of garlic, minced
2 teaspoons sugar
½ teaspoon salt
¼ cup olive oil or vegetable oil
3 tablespoons lemon juice
2 medium-size tomatoes, sliced thin

1 Combine beans, parsley, green pepper, onion, and garlic in a large bowl.
2 Mix sugar, salt, olive oil, and lemon juice in a cup; drizzle over bean mixture; toss lightly to mix. Let stand about an hour to season.
3 When ready to serve, line a shallow serving bowl or hollowed-out cabbage with romaine, if you wish. Arrange tomato slices around edge in bowl or cabbage; spoon bean mixture in center.

Twin-Bean Salad

Red kidney beans, green limas, and crisp vegetables team in this picnic salad

Makes 6 servings

2 packages (10 ounces each) frozen lima beans
2 tablespoons grated onion
   MUSTARD DRESSING (recipe follows)
2 cans (about 1 pound each) red kidney beans, drained
½ cup chopped celery
1 teaspoon garlic salt
1 teaspoon Worcestershire sauce
1 head of lettuce, shredded
1 can (9 ounces) ripe olives, drained
1 cup thinly sliced raw carrots

1 Cook lima beans in large saucepan, following label directions; drain; place in medium-size bowl. Stir in onion and ¼ cup MUSTARD DRESSING; cover; chill.

(continued)

2 Place drained kidney beans in second medium-size bowl. Stir in celery, garlic salt, Worcestershire sauce and ¼ cup MUSTARD DRESSING; cover; chill.
3 When ready to put salad together, place shredded lettuce in salad bowl. Spoon lima-bean and kidney-bean salads in 2 piles on top and separate with a row of olives. Edge lima beans with carrot slices; serve with remaining dressing.

MUSTARD DRESSING—Combine ¾ cup vegetable oil, ⅓ cup vinegar, 1 tablespoon prepared mustard and 1 teaspoon salt in small jar with tight-fitting cover. Shake to blend well. Makes about 1 cup.

Mexicali Salad Ring

What a refreshing combination of red beans, mandarin oranges and sweet onion!

Makes 4 to 6 servings

1 can (about 1 pound) red kidney beans
1 can (11 ounces) mandarin-orange segments
½ cup coarsely chopped sweet onion
¼ cup chopped parsley
¼ cup vegetable oil
2 tablespoons cider vinegar
1 teaspoon sugar
½ teaspoon salt
    Lettuce

1 Drain kidney beans and mandarin-orange segments. Toss onion with parsley in a small bowl; mix vegetable oil, vinegar, sugar and salt in a cup.
2 Line a shallow serving bowl with lettuce. Spoon beans in a ring around edge and mandarin-orange segments next to beans; pile onion mixture in center. Drizzle dressing over; toss lightly.

Guacamole Salad

A Mexican specialty becomes a delightful luncheon salad when served in tomato shells

Makes 6 to 8 servings

3 or 4 medium-size tomatoes
2 large firm ripe avocados
1 small onion, chopped (¼ cup)
1 green chili pepper, chopped fine
½ clove of garlic, minced
3 tablespoons mayonnaise or salad dressing
3 tablespoons lemon juice
1 teaspoon Worcestershire sauce
¼ teaspoon salt
    Dash of ground coriander
    Dash of cayenne
    Iceberg lettuce, shredded

1 Halve tomatoes crosswise; scoop out insides into a small bowl; dice. Turn tomatoes upside down on paper toweling to drain.
2 Halve avocados; peel and pit. Mash fruit with a fork in a medium-size bowl.
3 Stir in diced tomato and remaining ingredients, except lettuce. Spoon into tomato shells.
4 Arrange tomatoes on a lettuce-lined platter. Garnish each with several slices of pitted ripe olive and serve with corn chips, if you wish.

Green-and-Gold Salad

Bright avocado and sunny oranges make this salad refreshingly springlike

Makes 6 servings

1 small head of iceberg lettuce
1 medium-size ripe avocado, peeled and sliced
3 oranges, peeled and sectioned
1 small onion, sliced thin and separated into rings
    CELERY-SEED DRESSING (recipe follows)

1 Line 6 small salad bowls with lettuce leaves; break remaining into bite-size pieces, dividing evenly among bowls.
2 Arrange avocado slices, orange sections and onion rings on top.
3 Drizzle each with about 1 tablespoon CELERY-SEED DRESSING. Pass extra dressing, if you like.

CELERY-SEED DRESSING—Combine 1 teaspoon grated onion, ½ teaspoon salt, ½ teaspoon dry mustard, ½ teaspoon paprika, ½ teaspoon celery seeds, ½ cup vegetable oil, ¼ cup light corn syrup and 3 tablespoons cider vinegar in jar with tight-fitting cover. Shake until well blended. Keep covered in refrigerator. Shake again just before using. Makes about 1 cup.

HOW TO PICK TOP QUALITY GREENS:

Pick out fairly firm, medium-size heads of lettuce, as larger ones may be overgrown and tend to be slightly bitter. If you spot a reddish discoloration at stem end, don't be concerned. This is nature's way of sealing the cut that was made when the head was picked and trimmed.

For variety and interest, look for the less familiar regional or seasonal greens. Just a few examples are: Prize head lettuce with red-edged leaves; lamb's lettuce; fennel, or finochio, with its distinctive anise flavor; the tender young dandelion, mustard and beet greens, plus Swiss chard. You can cook these greens, of course, but don't miss out on the unusual flavor touches that just a few, chopped up, will add to a salad bowl.

If any varieties are brand-new to you, don't hesitate to ask your produce man about them. As a general rule, you can count on about 4 servings from a medium-size head of iceberg lettuce, or 1 pound of loose greens, or a 1½-pound head of cabbage.

Tomato Fan-Tans

Cucumbers in sour cream make both the filling and the dressing for this salad with a different twist

Makes 6 servings

½ cup dairy sour cream
1 teaspoon sugar
1 teaspoon salt
Dash of pepper
1 teaspoon prepared horseradish
2 tablespoons lemon juice
1 medium-size cucumber, sliced thin
1 small onion, sliced and separated into rings
6 medium-size tomatoes, peeled
Lettuce

1 Blend sour cream, sugar, salt, pepper, horseradish and lemon juice in a 1-cup measure. Pour over cucumber and onion slices in a small bowl; toss to mix; cover. Chill at least an hour to season and blend flavors.
2 Place tomatoes, stem end down, on cutting board; make 5 parallel cuts almost to bottom in each; spread apart slightly.
3 Place tomatoes on lettuce-lined salad plates; spoon the cucumber mixture into cuts.

Tomatoes Lutece

Juicy tomatoes, sliced and stacked into shape again, are marinated in a Parisian dressing

Makes 8 servings

8 firm ripe tomatoes, peeled
¼ cup chopped parsley
1 clove of garlic, crushed
1 teaspoon salt
1 teaspoon sugar
¼ teaspoon pepper
¼ cup olive oil or vegetable oil
2 tablespoons tarragon vinegar or cider vinegar
2 teaspoons prepared mustard

1 Cut out stem ends from tomatoes; slice each tomato crosswise into ½-inch-thick slices; reform into tomato shape again and place in shallow serving dish.
2 Combine remaining ingredients in small jar; cover; shake well; pour over tomatoes.
3 Cover lightly; let stand at room temperature at least 20 minutes before serving. (Any left over? Chill and serve the next day.)

Relish Tomatoes

So simple to fix, yet so tempting! Celery gives the dressing a pleasing crunch

Makes 8 servings

8 medium-size tomatoes, peeled
½ cup finely chopped parsley
½ cup finely chopped celery
1 small onion, finely chopped (¼ cup)
1 tablespoon sugar
1 teaspoon seasoned salt
½ teaspoon seasoned pepper
¼ teaspoon thyme
¼ teaspoon curry powder
1 cup olive oil or vegetable oil
⅓ cup wine vinegar or cider vinegar

1 Cut out stem ends of tomatoes; cut tomatoes

(continued)

into ½-inch-thick slices; arrange in layers in a large shallow serving bowl.
2 Combine remaining ingredients in a jar with tight-fitting lid; shake well to mix; pour over tomatoes; cover. Chill at least an hour to season and blend flavors. (Save any remaining dressing in bowl for tossing with green salad for another meal.)

Tomato Bouquet Salad

How pretty it looks with a nosegay of vegetables centering a ring of herb-seasoned tomatoes

Makes 8 servings

- 4 large ripe tomatoes, peeled and sliced ½ inch thick
- 1 tablespoon sugar
- 1 teaspoon salt
- 1 teaspoon leaf basil, crumbled
  Dash of pepper
- ½ small head curly endive, washed, dried and separated in leaves
- 1 small carrot, pared and cut in 3-inch-long thin sticks
- 1 small stalk celery, trimmed and cut in 3-inch-long thin sticks
- 4 pitted ripe olives
- ½ cup mayonnaise or salad dressing
- 2 tablespoons light cream or table cream
- 1 tablespoon lemon juice

1 Place tomato slices in a single layer in a shallow dish. Mix sugar, salt, basil and pepper in a cup; sprinkle over tomatoes; cover; chill until serving time.
2 When ready to serve, arrange tomato slices, overlapping, around edge of a shallow serving bowl; fill center with a "nest" of endive; tuck carrot and celery sticks into endive. Thread olives onto a kebab stick; place in center of salad.
3 Blend mayonnaise or salad dressing, cream and lemon juice in a small bowl.
4 Pass dressing separately to spoon over salad.

Tomato-Cucumber Cups

Jumbo tomatoes are hollowed out and filled brimful with tangy cucumber slices

Makes 6 servings

- 2 medium-size cucumbers
- 1 tablespoon finely cut fresh dill
- 3 tablespoons sugar
- ¼ teaspoon salt
- ⅛ teaspoon pepper
- ½ cup cider vinegar
- 6 large firm ripe tomatoes

1 Score cucumbers with a fork, then slice thin; set aside 6 slices for garnish. Place remaining in a medium-size bowl.
2 Combine dill, sugar, salt, pepper and vinegar in a cup; stir until sugar dissolves, then pour over cucumbers; toss lightly to mix; chill.
3 Cut a thin slice from bottom of each tomato; scoop out insides with a teaspoon. (Save pulp to add to soup.) Turn tomato cups upside down on paper toweling to drain. Chill cups and slices.
4 Just before serving, drain cucumbers; spoon into tomato cups; replace tops. Garnish each with a saved cucumber slice, a sprig of fresh dill and a radish threaded onto a wooden pick, if you wish. (To fix radishes, trim stem and root ends. Make about 6 cuts lengthwise into each, then make another cut just behind each line and lift out a narrow strip of peel.)

Calico Cups

Zippy Mexican-style corn fills hollowed-out canned tomatoes for this winter special

Makes 6 servings

- 2 cans (1 pound each) peeled whole tomatoes
- 1 can (12 ounces) Mexican-style corn
- ½ cup bottled oil-and-vinegar salad dressing
- 2 teaspoons grated onion
  Bibb lettuce

1 Empty tomatoes carefully into a large shallow pan. (There should be 3 in each can.) Lift out, one at a time, with a slotted spoon and drain on paper toweling, then gently scoop out insides. (Chill pulp and juice to add to soup or stew.) Set tomato cups in a pie plate.
2 Heat corn just to boiling in a small saucepan; drain. Stir in oil-and-vinegar dressing and onion; spoon into tomato cups; cover. Chill at least two hours to season and blend flavors.
3 When ready to serve, place each tomato on a lettuce-lined salad plate; top each with a sprig of parsley and serve with a dollop of your favorite mayonnaise or salad dressing, if you wish.

GARDEN FRESH SALADS • 83

Tomato-Shrimp Cups

Scooped-out tomatoes, heaped with "green" rice and shrimp salad, make this dish

Makes 4 servings

- 4 large tomatoes
  Seasoned salt
- 1 cup uncooked regular rice
- 4 tablespoons thin French dressing
- 1 pound frozen, deveined, shelled, raw shrimps
- 1 small onion, sliced
- ½ lemon, sliced
- ½ cup water
- ½ cup diced cucumber
- ½ cup diced green pepper
- 2 tablespoons chopped parsley
- 2 tablespoons chopped fresh dill
- 1 tablespoon chopped chives
- ½ teaspoon salt
- ½ cup mayonnaise or salad dressing

1 Cut off tops of tomatoes; scoop out insides with a teaspoon. (Save pulp for making stewed tomatoes or soup.) Sprinkle shells lightly with seasoned salt; turn upside down on plate to drain, then chill while making rice-shrimp filling.
2 Cook rice, following label directions; drain;

(continued)

Served up in a bed of lettuce, **Calico Cups** brighten any table or buffet.

Party-perfect, reserve **Tomato Cucumber Cups** for a special occasion.

spoon into a medium-size bowl. Drizzle 2 tablespoons of the French dressing over; toss lightly; cover. Let stand at room temperature while cooking and seasoning shrimps. (Save remaining French dressing for Step 4.)
3 Combine shrimps, onion, lemon and water in a large frying pan; cover; simmer 20 minutes, or until shrimps are tender. Lift out with a slotted spoon; place in a medium-size bowl.
4 When cool enough to handle, set 4 large shrimps aside for topping cups in Step 6; halve remaining. Drizzle saved 2 tablespoons French dressing over; toss to mix well; cover. Chill at least an hour to season and blend flavors.
5 Just before serving, stir shrimps, cucumber, green pepper, parsley, dill, chives and salt into rice; fold in mayonnaise or salad dressing until well blended.
6 Pile into tomato cups; garnish each with a saved whole shrimp and an additional cucumber slice, held in place with a wooden pick.

Tomato Cups Provençale

The secret lies in the soft blending of chives and anchovy

Makes 6 servings

- 6 medium-size potatoes, pared and diced
- ½ cup bottled oil-and-vinegar dressing
- 6 large tomatoes
- 2 hard-cooked eggs, shelled and diced
- 1 can (2 ounces) anchovy fillets, drained and chopped
- ¼ cup sliced pitted ripe olives
- 3 tablespoons chopped parsley
- 1 tablespoon finely cut chives

1 Cook potatoes, covered, in boiling salted water in a large saucepan 15 minutes, or until tender; drain. Return potatoes to pan and shake over low heat until dry and fluffy. Place in a large bowl; drizzle oil-and-vinegar dressing over top. Let stand at least an hour to season.
2 Peel tomatoes, if you wish. Cut a thin slice from top of each, then scoop out insides with a teaspoon, being careful not to break shells. Turn tomato cups upside down on paper toweling to drain; chill.
3 Fold eggs, anchovies, olives, parsley and chives into potato mixture; spoon into chilled tomato cups. Garnish each with two ripe olives threaded onto a wooden pick and serve on lettuce-lined plates, if you wish.

Coleslaw-Tomato Cups

Each bright red cup holds a rich coleslaw filling

Makes 6 servings

- 1 small head of cabbage, weighing about 1½ pounds
- 2 tablespoons sugar
- 6 medium-size tomatoes
- 2 tablespoons mayonnaise or salad dressing
- 2 tablespoons cream
- 2 tablespoons lemon juice
- ½ teaspoon salt
- Dash of pepper

1 Quarter cabbage; core; shred fine. Place in a large bowl.
2 Sprinkle sugar over cabbages; toss lightly to mix; cover. Chill at least 30 minutes to crisp.
3 While cabbage chills, cut a thin slice from top of each tomato; scoop out insides. Turn tomato cups upside down in a pie plate to drain; chill.
4 Blend mayonnaise or salad dressing, cream, lemon juice, salt and pepper in a cup.
5 Drain cabbage; drizzle dressing over top. Toss lightly to mix. Spoon into tomato cups. Serve on lettuce-lined salad plates, if you wish.

Tomato-Aspic Crown

A shimmering mold, filled with goodness

Makes 6 servings

- 2 envelopes unflavored gelatin
- 3 cups tomato-juice cocktail
- 1 can (8 ounces) tomato sauce
- 2 teaspoons Worcestershire sauce
- 1 large cucumber
- ½ cup bottled oil-and-vinegar salad dressing
- ½ teaspoon salt

1 Soften gelatin in 1½ cups of the tomato-juice cocktail in a medium-size saucepan. Heat, stirring constantly, until gelatin dissolves; remove from heat.
2 Stir in remaining tomato-juice cocktail and tomato and Worcestershire sauces. Pour into a 4-cup mold. Chill several hours, or until firm.
3 Slice cucumber thin; place in a shallow dish. Drizzle with dressing; sprinkle with salt; cover. Chill at least an hour to season.
4 When ready to serve, unmold onto a large serving plate.
5 Drain liquid from cucumber. Overlap slices in a ring around salad.

Spinach-Tomato Salad Mimosa

Pretty, nutritious, and inexpensive!

Makes 6 servings

- 1 package (10 ounces) fresh spinach
- 1 can (about 1 pound) whole tomatoes
- 1 hard-cooked egg, shelled
- 1 tablespoon sugar
- 1 teaspoon salt
- ¼ teaspoon pepper
- 2 tablespoons cider vinegar
- 1 tablespoon water

1 Remove coarse stems from spinach; break leaves into bite-size pieces in salad bowl.
2 Empty tomatoes into a shallow dish; set the largest, most perfect one aside for garnish. Chop remaining coarsely; add to spinach. (Use juice from can for beverage.)
3 Dice white of egg and add to spinach. Sieve yolk; pile into top of saved whole tomato.
4 Mix sugar, salt, pepper, vinegar, and water in a cup; pour over salad; toss to mix well. Garnish with egg-topped whole tomato.

Tomato-Kraut Cups

Scooped-out tomatoes are filled brimful with tangy seasoned sauerkraut

Makes 6 servings

- 1 can (about 1 pound) sauerkraut
- 6 medium-size firm ripe tomatoes
- 3 tablespoons vegetable oil
- 1 tablespoon cider vinegar
- 1 tablespoon catsup
- 1 small onion, grated
- 1 teaspoon sugar
- ⅛ teaspoon salt
- ½ teaspoon Worcestershire sauce
  Shredded lettuce

1 Drain sauerkraut; pat dry between sheets of paper toweling. Chop coarsely and place in large bowl.
2 Wash tomatoes and cut off tops; scoop out insides with teaspoon. Turn tomato cups upside down to drain, then chill. Chop tomato pulp; add to sauerkraut.
3 Combine vegetable oil, vinegar, catsup, onion, sugar, salt, and Worcestershire sauce in a cup; pour over sauerkraut mixture; toss lightly to mix. Let stand 30 minutes to blend flavors.
4 When ready to serve, heap sauerkraut mixture in tomato cups; place on individual serving plates lined with shredded lettuce.

Caraway Cabbage Toss

An easy-to-do extravaganza

Makes 12 servings

- 1 medium-size head cabbage
- ⅔ cup vegetable oil
- ⅓ cup vinegar
- 1 tablespoon caraway seeds
- 1 teaspoon sugar
- ½ teaspoon salt
  Dash of pepper
- 3 medium-size apples
  Large romaine leaves

1 Trim outer leaves from cabbage; quarter head and cut out core. Shred cabbage fine. (There will be about 9 cups.) Place in a large bowl.
2 Combine vegetable oil, vinegar, caraway seeds, sugar, salt, and pepper in a jar with a tight-fitting lid; shake well to mix. Pour over cabbage; toss lightly; cover. Chill several hours.
3 When ready to serve, quarter apples; core; slice thin crosswise. Set aside a few slices for garnish; toss remainder with cabbage mixture. Spoon into a romaine-lined salad bowl; overlap remaining apple slices on top.

Cabbage Relish Salads

A great salad for slimmers, this crisply different coleslaw made with shredded Chinese cabbage and carrots

Makes 6 servings, 34 calories each

- 1 small head Chinese cabbage
- 2 large carrots
- 3 tablespoons low-calorie mayonnaise
- 2 tablespoons skim milk
- 1 tablespoon cider vinegar
- ¼ teaspoon dry mustard
- ¼ teaspoon salt
- ⅛ teaspoon pepper
  Granulated or liquid no-calorie sweetener
- 6 large lettuce leaves

(continued)

1 Shred cabbage fine; wash and drain well. Place in a large bowl. Pare carrots and shred; add to cabbage.
2 Blend mayonnaise, milk, vinegar, mustard, salt, and pepper in a cup; stir in your favorite no-calorie sweetener, using the equivalent of 2 tablespoons sugar. Pour over cabbage mixture; toss lightly to mix.
3 Line 6 individual salad bowls with lettuce; spoon cabbage mixture in centers.

Onion-Ring Salad Bowl

Simply toss crisp greens and nippy onions with zesty dressing to make this favorite

Makes 8 servings

1 medium-size head of iceberg lettuce
1 medium-size head of romaine
4 small white onions, peeled, sliced thin, and separated into rings
1 envelope Italian salad-dressing mix
Vegetable oil
Cider vinegar

1 Break lettuce and romaine leaves into bite-size pieces in large salad bowl. Top with onion rings.
2 Prepare Italian salad-dressing mix with vegetable oil, vinegar, and water, following label directions. Pour ⅓ cup over salad; toss to mix well. Serve at once. (Store remaining dressing in covered jar in refrigerator for another salad.)

Apple-Celery Salad

This favorite looks extra inviting when served in bowls lined with apple slices

Makes 6 servings

3 medium-size tart apples
1½ cups sliced celery
½ cup chopped walnuts
¼ cup mayonnaise or salad dressing
2 teaspoons sugar
Dash of ground allspice
1 teaspoon lemon juice

1 Pare, quarter, core, and dice 2 apples. (Save remaining apple for Step 3.) Place in medium-size bowl; stir in celery and walnuts.
2 Blend remaining ingredients in 1-cup measure; pour over apple mixture; toss lightly to mix.
3 Quarter and core saved apple; cut into thin slices.
4 Fill individual salad bowls with apple mixture, dividing evenly; garnish with a stand-up ring of apple slices around edges. Top each with a halved walnut, if you wish.

Served in individual bowls or in a large salad dish, **Apple-Celery Salad** add sparkle to any table.

Sunday-Supper Salad

This cheese and vegetable salad has a surprise flavor ingredient . . . pretzels

Makes 8 servings.

- 1 small head iceberg lettuce, broken into bite-size pieces
- 1 small head romaine, broken into bite-size pieces
- 1 large cucumber, pared and sliced
- 1 large green pepper, halved, seeded and sliced
- 10 ounces sharp Cheddar cheese, cut into ¼-inch cubes
- 1 package (8 ounces) sliced caraway cheese, cut in thin strips
- 1 teaspoon coriander seeds
- 1 teaspoon cumin seeds
- 6 peppercorns
- 1 egg
- ½ cup bottled Italian salad dressing
- 1 cup broken pretzels

1 Place lettuce and romaine in a large salad bowl; top with cucumber and green pepper. Pile Cheddar-cheese cubes in a mound in center; place caraway-cheese strips in a ring around Cheddar.
2 Crush coriander and cumin seeds and peppercorns; sprinkle over salad mixture. (To speed the job, fold seeds and peppercorns in a double-thick sheet of wax paper; crush with a rolling pin.)
3 Place egg in boiling water in a small saucepan; cover; remove from heat. Let stand only 2 minutes.
4 Break egg into a cup, then place in center of salad mixture; drizzle dressing over all; add pretzels. Toss to mix well.

Macaroni and Mozzarella Salad

Pasta needn't be hot to be good, as this savory Italian-style salad proves. It couldn't be easier or more economical to make

Makes 6 servings.

- 1 cup uncooked elbow macaroni
- ½ cup mayonnaise or salad dressing
- ¼ teaspoon leaf oregano, crumbled
  Pinch leaf thyme
- 1 teaspoon dry mustard
- 2 teaspoons salt
- ⅛ teaspoon white pepper
- 2 tablespoons minced onion
- 2 tablespoons minced green pepper
- 1 tablespoon minced, drained pimiento
- ¾ cup finely diced celery
- ⅓ cup finely diced, peeled, seeded cucumber
- 1 cup coarsely shredded mozzarella, Swiss or Cheddar cheese (about 4 ounces)
- 3 hard-cooked eggs, chopped

1 Cook macaroni by package directions until firm-tender, adding a drop of vegetable oil to the cooking water to keep macaroni from sticking to itself; drain.
2 Meanwhile, mix together mayonnaise, oregano, thyme, mustard, salt, white pepper, onion, green pepper and pimiento.
3 Place macaroni, celery and cucumber in a large bowl. Add mayonnaise mixture and stir gently to mix. Add cheese and eggs and toss just enough to mix. Chill for about 2 to 3 hours before serving.

Peruvian Potato Salad

This salad is one chili-pepper fans will love

Makes 8 servings.

- 6 medium-size potatoes, pared and cubed (6 cups)
- 2 hard-cooked eggs, shelled
- 1 cup shredded Cheddar cheese (4 ounces)
- 1 small onion, chopped fine (¼ cup)
- 1 jalapeño or green chili pepper, chopped fine
- 1 teaspoon salt
- 2 tablespoons olive or vegetable oil
- ½ cup light cream
  Iceberg lettuce

1 Cook potatoes in boiling salted water in a large saucepan 15 minutes, or until tender; drain. Return potatoes to pan and shake over low heat until dry and fluffy. Place in a large bowl.
2 While potatoes cook, mash eggs in a small bowl; stir in cheese, onion, pepper and salt. Slowly stir in olive oil until well-blended, then add cream. Pour over warm potatoes, toss until evenly coated.
3 Chill about an hour to season. Serve in a large lettuce-lined salad bowl.

Egg and Swiss Cheese Salad

It's tangy egg salad combined with cheese

Makes 4 servings.

- 6 hard-cooked eggs, coarsely chopped
- 6 ounces Swiss cheese slices, cut in slivers
- ⅓ cup mayonnaise or salad dressing
- 1 tablespoon mustard with horseradish
- ¼ cup chopped green pepper
- 2 tablespoons chopped pimiento
- ½ teaspoon salt
- ⅛ teaspoon pepper
  Salad greens

1 Combine eggs, cheese, mayonnaise or salad dressing, mustard, green pepper, pimiento, salt and pepper in a large bowl. Toss lightly to coat. Chill.
2 Serve on crisp salad greens with a sprinkling of chopped chives, if you wish.

Two-Cheese Salad

Two kinds of cheese combine with two varieties of greens to make a double-good salad

Makes 6 servings.

- 1 small head romaine
- 1 small head iceberg lettuce
- ¼ pound sharp Cheddar cheese, cubed
- ¼ pound Monterey Jack cheese, cubed or ¼ pound Muenster cheese, cubed
- 6 small thin carrots, trimmed and scraped
- 6 white radishes, trimmed and scraped
  PIQUANT DRESSING (recipe follows)

1 Break romaine and lettuce into bite-size pieces in individual salad bowls, leaving a shallow well in center of each. Arrange cheese cubes around well.
2 Bunch carrots and radishes, tip ends up, to form a bouquet; place in center well. (Cheese cubes will hold bouquet in place.)
3 Serve PIQUANT DRESSING and have each person add his own dressing.
  PIQUANT DRESSING—Combine ⅔ cup salad oil, ⅓ cup wine vinegar or cider vinegar, 2 teaspoons sugar, ½ teaspoon dry mustard and ½ teaspoon salt in jar with tight-fitting cover. Shake well to mix; chill; then shake again just before serving. Makes 1 cup.

Confetti Cauliflower Bowl

Here's an unusual approach to making salad—the crisp vegetables are part of the dressing

Makes 6 servings.

- 1 large head iceberg lettuce
- ½ head small cauliflower
- ½ cup bottled Italian salad dressing
- 2 tablespoons minced radishes
- 2 tablespoons minced carrot
- 2 tablespoons minced green onion
- ½ cup shredded Cheddar cheese (about 2 ounces)

1 Trim lettuce; wash; drain. Wrap in towel to absorb moisture. Chill several hours.
2 Trim and remove core from cauliflower; separate into flowerets. Wash; drain; dry. Cut each floweret lengthwise into very thin slices (about 1½ cups).
3 Mix salad dressing, radishes, carrot and green onion in a pie plate; add cauliflower; turn to coat well. Chill, turning several times, at least 1 hour.
4 When ready to serve, break lettuce into bite-size pieces in a large salad bowl. (You should have about 6 cups.) Sprinkle cheese over top. Spoon dressing with vegetables over all. Toss lightly to coat.

Seaway Salad Bowl

Brimful with color and flavor, accompany any entree with this jaunty salad

Makes 6 servings

- 1 medium-size head romaine, broken in bite-size pieces
- 1 large sweet red pepper, halved, seeded, and cut in thin strips
- 1 small head chicory or curly endive, separated into leaves
- 1 large sweet onion, peeled, sliced thin, and separated into rings
  Bottled Italian salad dressing

1 Layer romaine, red pepper, chicory, and onion rings into a salad bowl.
2 Just before serving, drizzle with about ¼ cup Italian dressing; toss lightly to mix.

Pickled Beets

Beets with a tart flavor, from Sweden

Makes 6 servings

1 can (1 pound) sliced beets
1 tablespoon mixed pickling spices
1 tablespoon cider vinegar

1 Drain liquid from beets into a small saucepan; add pickling spices and vinegar. Heat to boiling; lower heat; simmer 5 minutes.
2 Place beets in a small bowl. Strain beet liquid over and chill several hours.

Tart Spinach Salad

It's a hot salad specialty of a famous Hollywood restaurant. Try it—it's deliciously different

Makes 8 servings

½ pound fresh spinach
6 slices (from a 6-ounce package) Italian assortment cold cuts, diced
⅓ cup vegetable oil
¼ cup cider vinegar
1 teaspoon sugar
½ teaspoon seasoned salt
2 teaspoons soy sauce
1 teaspoon prepared mustard

1 Remove stems and any large ribs from spinach; wash leaves; drain well, then tear into bite-size pieces. (You should have about 12 cups.) Place in large salad bowl.
2 Sauté diced cold cuts in vegetable oil just until heated through in medium-size frying pan. Stir in remaining ingredients; heat, stirring constantly, just to boiling.
3 Pour at once over spinach; toss to coat all leaves well. Serve immediately.

Cool Cucumber Salad

One taste and we think you'll agree this way with cucumbers is most refreshing

Makes 8 to 10 servings

3 medium-size cucumbers
3 teaspoons salt
1 cup (8-ounce container) plain yogurt
1 tablespoon vegetable oil
2 tablespoons chopped parsley
¼ teaspoon pepper
1 medium-size head of iceberg lettuce, broken into bite-size pieces (about 6 cups)

1 Pare cucumbers; slice thin (you should have about 4 cups). Mix with 2 teaspoons salt in medium-size bowl. (Save remaining teaspoon salt for Step 2.) Cover bowl; let stand 30 to 45 minutes. Pour into a strainer; let drain, then squeeze out as much liquid as possible.
2 Mix yogurt, vegetable oil, parsley, saved 1 teaspoon salt and pepper in same bowl; stir in well-drained cucumbers; chill until serving time.
3 Fill a large salad bowl with lettuce; pour cucumber dressing over; toss to coat greens well.

Summer's Best Green Salad

Peak-of-the-season greens and green onions, tossed with a low-calorie tomato dressing, make this a family favorite

Makes 6 servings

1 small head of romaine
1 small head of leaf lettuce
3 green onions, sliced
1 envelope French salad-dressing mix
¾ cup fresh or canned tomato juice
¼ cup cider vinegar
2 tablespoons water

1 Break romaine and lettuce leaves into bite-size pieces in a large bowl. (There should be about 6 cups.) Add onions.
2 Combine salad-dressing mix, tomato juice, vinegar and water in a jar with tight-fitting lid; shake well to mix.
3 Drizzle about ¼ cup over greens; toss to coat well. Pass remaining dressing, if you wish.

Parsley Chiffonade Salad

Crisp green parsley gives this salad a pungent flavor that men especially like

Makes 6 servings

1 large bunch of parsley
4 hard-cooked eggs, coarsely chopped
3 medium-size tomatoes, peeled and diced
1 can (4 ounces) sardines, drained and cut up
VEGETABLE DRESSING (recipe follows)

(continued)

GARDEN FRESH SALADS

1 Wash parsley, remove stems, and dry well on paper toweling (you should have about 6 cups). Place in large salad bowl; sprinkle eggs, tomatoes and sardines over.
2 Pour VEGETABLE DRESSING over parsley mixture, tossing to coat salad well.

Vegetable Dressing

Makes ⅓ cup

- ¼ cup olive oil or vegetable oil
- 2 tablespoons wine vinegar or cider vinegar
- 6 radishes, grated
- ½ clove of garlic, minced
- ½ teaspoon sugar
- ½ teaspoon paprika
- ⅛ teaspoon pepper

Combine all ingredients in small jar with tight-fitting cover; shake well just before serving.

Green Salad with Grapes and Walnuts

Serve fruit and cheese the salad way! Orange dressing is refreshingly tart and pleasing

Makes 6 servings

- 4 heads Bibb lettuce
- 1 cup cubed Swiss cheese
- 1 firm ripe peach, halved, pitted and sliced
- 1 can (about 9 ounces) pineapple tidbits, drained
- ½ cup purple grapes, halved and seeded
- ¼ cup walnut halves
- GINGER ORANGE DRESSING (recipe follows)

1 Cut core from each head of lettuce and separate into leaves; wash well; dry thoroughly. Place in a large salad bowl with cheese, peach slices, pineapple, grapes and walnuts.
2 Drizzle part of the GINGER ORANGE DRESSING on top; toss lightly to mix. Serve with remaining dressing.

GINGER ORANGE DRESSING—Combine ¼ cup vegetable oil, 2 tablespoons thawed frozen concentrated orange juice (from a 6-ounce can), 1 tablespoon honey, ¼ teaspoon salt and ⅛ teaspoon ground ginger in a small jar with a tight-fitting lid; shake well to mix. Makes about ½ cup.

Continental Green Salad

Crushed coriander seeds give this simple salad a refreshingly different flavor

Makes 6 to 8 servings

- 8 cups broken mixed salad greens (romaine, leaf and iceberg lettuce)

Turn salad-time into fruit-time with **Green Salad with Grapes and Walnuts.**

1 small yellow squash, sliced thin
1 small sweet red pepper, seeded and sliced into thin rings
1 small red onion, sliced thin and separated into rings
¼ pound sharp Cheddar cheese, cubed
½ cup olive oil or vegetable oil
¼ cup wine vinegar or cider vinegar
  Coriander seeds, crushed
  Salt and pepper

1 Fill a large salad bowl with greens, squash slices, red-pepper and onion rings and cheese cubes; toss lightly. (This can be done ahead. Then slide bowl into a large transparent plastic bag, or cover with foil or transparent wrap, and place in the refrigerator to keep chilled until serving time.)
2 Serve salad in individual bowls for each to dress his own with oil and vinegar, mixed; a tiny sprinkling of crushed coriander seeds; and salt and pepper.
Note—If you have any greens left over, wrap loosely in transparent wrap or foil and save for a next-day's meal, they'll keep freshly crisp if they have no dressing on them.

White Mountain Radish Bowl

Lots of tangy radishes are seasoned with a sweet-sour dressing for this delightful variation on tossed salad

                    Makes 6 servings

6 cups broken escarole or lettuce
4 bunches radishes, trimmed and sliced thin (about 4 cups)
8 slices bacon, diced
2 tablespoons sugar
2 tablespoons wine vinegar or cider vinegar
2 tablespoons water
1 teaspoon seasoned salt

1 Place escarole or lettuce in a large salad bowl; mound sliced radishes on top.
2 Sauté bacon until crisp in a medium-size frying pan; remove and drain on paper toweling.
3 Pour drippings into a cup, then measure 4 tablespoonfuls back into pan; stir in sugar, wine vinegar or cider vinegar, water and seasoned salt. Heat to boiling; remove from heat.
4 Pour over radishes in bowl; add bacon; toss lightly to mix.

GARDEN FRESH SALADS • 91

Old-Fashioned Cabbage Slaw

Thinly sliced apple and a little fennel seed highlight cabbage salad

                    Makes 8 servings

1 head cabbage (about 2½ pounds)
½ cup sugar
3 teaspoons salt
1 teaspoon fennel seeds, crushed
2 medium-size tart red apples
2 tablespoons lemon juice
1 cup mayonnaise or salad dressing
½ cup dairy sour cream

1 Trim cabbage; quarter; shred fine. (You will have about 10 cups.) Combine with sugar, salt and fennel seed in a large salad bowl; toss to mix well; let stand at room temperature, tossing occasionally, about ½ hour; drain, discarding liquid.
2 Meanwhile, quarter and core apples (do not pare); cut into very thin slices; toss with lemon juice in a small bowl.
3 Just before serving, blend mayonnaise or salad dressing and sour cream in a small bowl. Toss apples with drained cabbage; pour dressing over cabbage mixture; toss until evenly coated.

Chinese Slaw

Toss refreshing oranges and crisp Chinese cabbage with a ginger-flavored dressing

                    Makes 8 servings

8 cups shredded Chinese cabbage (1 small head)
4 large oranges
2 tablespoons cut chives
¾ cup mayonnaise or salad dressing
2 tablespoons sugar
½ teaspoon ground ginger
2 tablespoons lemon juice

1 Place cabbage in a large salad bowl; pare and section oranges over a small bowl to catch juice; reserve. Pile orange sections in center of cabbage; sprinkle chives over all.
2 Blend mayonnaise or salad dressing, sugar, ginger, lemon juice and 2 tablespoons of the reserved orange juice in a small bowl.
3 Just before serving, pour dressing over salad; toss lightly until evenly coated.

Farmer's Slaw

Marinated shredded yellow turnip and mellow pears are a surprise salad combo

Makes 8 servings

- ⅔ cup vegetable oil
- ⅓ cup cider vinegar
- 3 tablespoons sugar
- 1 teaspoon salt
- ¼ teaspoon ground mace
- ¼ teaspoon dry mustard
- ¼ teaspoon paprika
- 4 cups shredded yellow turnip (1 small turnip, about 1½ pounds)
- 2 large fresh pears
- 2 teaspoons lemon juice
- 6 cups finely cut romaine

1 Combine oil, vinegar, sugar, salt, mace, mustard and paprika in a jar with a tight lid; shake well to mix; pour dressing over turnip in a medium-size bowl; cover; chill 1 hour to season.
2 Pare pears; quarter, core and dice. Toss with lemon juice in a small bowl; cover; chill until ready to serve.
3 Just before serving, place romaine in a large salad bowl; arrange turnip and dressing around edge; spoon pears in center; toss until evenly coated.

Triple Vegetable Slaw

Pungent yellow turnip and sweet red beet give color and zing to this winter salad

Makes 6 servings

- 4 cups finely shredded cabbage
- 6 tablespoons NO-COOK "BOILED" DRESSING (recipe follows)
- 2 cups shredded pared yellow turnip
- 1 small red apple, quartered, cored and chopped
- ½ cup shredded pared beet

1 Toss cabbage with 3 tablespoons of the dressing in a medium-size bowl. Toss turnip and apple with remaining 3 tablespoons dressing in a second medium size bowl.
2 Spoon cabbage mixture into a salad bowl; mound turnip-apple mixture on top. Garnish with a cone of shredded beet.

No-Cook "Boiled" Dressing

Its flavor is just sweet and tart enough. And it keeps perfectly in the refrigerator

Makes about 2½ cups

- 1 egg
- 1 tablespoon dry mustard
- 1 teaspoon salt
- ½ teaspoon paprika
  Dash of cayenne
- 1 cup cider vinegar
- 1 can (14 or 15 ounces) sweetened condensed milk
- 4 tablespoons (½ stick) butter or margarine, melted

1 Beat egg until thick in a medium-size bowl. Beat in mustard, salt, paprika and cayenne; slowly beat in vinegar.
2 Stir in condensed (*not* evaporated) milk and melted butter or margarine; beat again until well blended.
3 Store leftover dressing in a covered jar in the refrigerator.

Classic Caesar Salad

A favorite salad with the classic touch

Makes 6 servings

- 4 tablespoons olive oil
- 3 tablespoons wine vinegar or cider vinegar
- 2 tablespoons lemon juice
- 1 clove of garlic, minced
- 1 teaspoon salt
- ⅛ teaspoon coarsely ground pepper
- 1 large head of romaine
- 1 egg
- ¼ cup freshly grated Parmesan cheese
- 1 can anchovy fillets
- 1½ cups GOLDEN CROUTONS (recipe follows)

1 Combine olive oil, vinegar, lemon juice, garlic, salt and pepper in a large salad bowl.
2 Separate romaine leaves; wash and dry well. (This is important so that moisture does not dilute dressing). Cut out any coarse ribs; then break leaves in bite-size pieces into bowl. (You should have about 12 cups).
3 Place egg in boiling water in small saucepan; cover; remove from heat and let stand 1 minute to coddle. Remove from water at once.
4 Top greens with Parmesan cheese and an-

Always select fresh vegetables that are plump and ripe.

chovies (more or less to suit your taste, as they are salty); break coddled egg over all.
5 Toss salad, spooning from bottom of bowl each time, until greens are evenly coated with dressing. Sprinkle with GOLDEN CROUTONS; toss to coat well.

GOLDEN CROUTONS—Cut 3 slices slightly dry bread into small cubes; spread in a single layer in a shallow baking pan. Bake in a slow oven (300°) 15 minutes or until crisply golden. Makes 1½ cups.

Oriental Toss

Popular foods of the Far East are layered into a bowl, then topped with a curry-sparked dressing

Makes 8 servings

- 2 cans (1 pound each) bean sprouts, drained
- ¼ cup thin French dressing
- 1 teaspoon soy sauce
- 2 cups broken fresh spinach
- 1 small green pepper, stemmed, seeded and cut in thin rings
- 1 can (1 pound, 4 ounces) pineapple chunks
- 1 can (5 ounces) water chestnuts, drained and sliced
- ¼ cup chopped peanuts
  CURRY DRESSING (recipe follows)

1 Place bean sprouts in a medium-size bowl; drizzle with French dressing and soy sauce; toss to mix; cover. Chill, tossing several times, at least an hour to season and blend flavors.
2 Just before serving, place spinach in a large shallow salad bowl. Drain bean sprouts; layer with green-pepper rings over spinach in bowl.
3 Drain syrup from pineapple chunks into a cup; layer fruit and water chestnuts over green pepper. Sprinkle with peanuts.
4 Spoon CURRY DRESSING over all; toss lightly with two forks until well coated.

CURRY DRESSING—Blend ½ cup mayonnaise or salad dressing, 2 tablespoons of the saved pineapple syrup and ¼ teaspoon curry powder until smooth in a small bowl; chill. Makes about ½ cup.

Calico Pepper Baskets

A simple cutting trick turns green and red peppers into pretty "dishes" for crisp coleslaw

Makes 6 servings

- 8 cups finely shredded cabbage (about 2 pounds)
- 2 tablespoons sugar
- 3 medium-size sweet red peppers
- 3 medium-size green peppers
- ½ cup shredded carrot
- 2 tablespoons mayonnaise or salad dressing
- 2 tablespoons lemon juice
- 2 tablespoons light cream or table cream
- ¼ teaspoon salt
- ⅛ teaspoon pepper
- Lettuce

1 Place cabbage in a large bowl; sprinkle with sugar; toss lightly to mix; cover. Chill at least 30 minutes to crisp and mellow cabbage.
2 Make pepper baskets this way: Holding each pepper stem end down, mark a guideline around center with wooden picks. Then mark a ½-inch-wide strip across top for basket handle. Cut out sections between marks. Scoop out seeds and membrane; chill peppers. Chop cut pieces fine for next step.
3 Just before serving, drain cabbage. Add carrot and ¼ cup of the chopped green pepper and 1 tablespoon of the chopped red pepper.
4 Blend mayonnaise or salad dressing, lemon juice, cream, salt and pepper in a cup; pour over cabbage; toss to coat cabbage evenly.
5 Spoon into pepper baskets; place on lettuce-lined salad plates. Garnish each basket with a carrot curl, if you wish. (To make, shave long thin strips from a pared carrot with a vegetable parer. Wind each around fingertip; fasten with a wooden pick. Place in a bowl of ice and water until they're curled and crisp.)

Ruffled Squash Boats

Seasoned zucchini slices and red kidney beans sail to the table in scooped-out yellow-squash halves

Makes 6 servings

- 3 large yellow squashes, trimmed and halved lengthwise
- 4 small zucchini, trimmed and sliced ¼ inch thick
- 1 can (about 1 pound) red kidney beans, drained
- ¾ cup bottled Italian salad dressing
- 2 tablespoons chopped parsley
- Lettuce

1 Cook yellow-squash halves in boiling salted water in a large frying pan 12 minutes, or until crisply tender; lift out with a slotted spoon. Carefully scoop out center of each; turn shells upside down on paper toweling to drain. Place in a single layer in a shallow dish.
2 Cook zucchini in boiling salted water in a medium-size saucepan 8 minutes, or until crisply tender; drain. Place in a pie plate. Place kidney beans in a second pie plate.
3 Mix salad dressing and parsley in a 1-cup measure; drizzle ¼ cup over each of the squashes and beans; cover. Chill at least an hour to season and blend flavors.
4 When ready to serve, arrange zucchini slices, overlapping, in yellow-squash halves on lettuce-lined salad plates; spoon kidney beans in center. Garnish with sprigs of parsley, if you wish.

INDEX

A-B

Antipasto Platter, 17
Apple Celery Salad, 86
Apple Salad, Cottage, 62
Apple Salad Cups, 63
Asparagus, Roquefort Mousse with Ham, Pineapple and, 11
Aspic-Bean Molds, 43
Aspic, Chicken Mousse in, 23
Aspic Crown, Tomato-, 84
Aspic, Dilled Shrimp in, 31
Aspic, Salmon in, 29
Avocado Chip Cream, 51
Avocado Appetizers, 55
Avocado Salad, and Chicken, 8
Avocado Salad Bowl, Orange-, 58
Baked Potato Salad, Bavarian, 12
Beanie Ring, Boston, 43
Bean Bowl, Italian, 76
Bean Bowl, Mustard, 79
Bean Molds, Aspic-, 43
Bean Salad Bowl, Double, 76
Bean Salad, Chili-, 77
Bean Salad, Picnic, 77
Bean Salad, Twin, 79
Beans, Sweet-Sour Brown, 79
Beet Mold, Lemon, 44
Beets, Pickled, 89
Berry Mold, Lemon, 45
Blue Cheese French Dressing, 21
Boeuf à la Mode en Gelee, 32
"Boiled" Dressing, No-Cook, 92
Bouillabaisse Salad, 13
Buffet Mold, 42

C

Cabbage Relish Salads, 85
Cabbage Slaw, Old-Fashioned, 91
Cabbage Toss, Caraway, 85
Caesar Salad, Classic, 92
Calico Cups, 82
Camembert Cream, 63
Cantaloupe Coupe, 54
Cantaloupe-Fruit Coupe, 50
Caraway Cabbage Toss, 85
Carrot Curls, 69
Cauliflower Bowl, Confetti, 88
Celery Seed Dressing, 80
Cheese Dressing, Creamy Blue, 21
Cheese Fluff, 46
Cheese Salad, Two-, 88
Chef's Salad, 10
Chef's Salad, Lazy Susan, 1-
Chef's Salad, The Perfect, 9
Chef's Salad, Seafood, 68
Chicken and Avocado Salad, 8
Chicken Coronet, curried-, 40
Chicken Indienne, 27
Chicken Loaf, Jellied, 36
Chicken Mousse in Aspic, 23
Chicken Salad Deluxe, 15
Chicken Salad Mimosa, 18
Chicken Supper Salad, Barbecued, 16
Chili Sauce, Tomato and Green, 8
Coleslaw-Relish Mold, 44
Coleslaw-Tomato Cups, 84
Corned Beef, Sauerkraut Salad with, 9

Corned-Beef Ring, Molded, 32
Cornucopia Salad Bowl, 16
Cottage Cheese Snow, 20
Crab Know-How, 70
Crab Louis Pillets, 69
Crab Salad Bowls, King, 70
Crab Salad, Louisiana, 70
Crab Salad with Louis-Dressing Mold, Patio, 26
Cranberry Crown, 33
Cranberry Salad, Cape Cod, 35
Creamy Dressing, 32
Croutons, Golden, 93
Cucumber-Cream Mold, 42
Cucumber Diadem, Shrimp-, 37
Cucumber-Rice Ring with Stuffed Lobster, 25
Cucumber Salad, Cool, 89
Cucumber Salad, Pineapple-, 61
Curry a la Creme, 19
Curry Dressing, 93

D-G

Double Salad Jumbo, 18
Dressing (see also Sauce), 7, 8, 10, 14, 17, **19-22,** 27, 32, 44, 49, 50, 54, 60, 63, 69, 70, 80, 90, 93
Egg Daisies, Stuffed, 76
Egg and Swiss Cheese Salad, 88
Egg Mold, Sun-Gold, 35
Eggs, Tomalley-Stuffed, 72
Eggs, Stuffed, 76
Fassoul Iahnia, 79
French Dressing, Blue Cheese, 21
French Dressing, Tangy, 21
French Dressing, Tomato, 21
Fruit-Peel Sparkles, 56
Fruit Platter, Chefette, 59
Fruit Salad, Gold Coast, 55
Fruit Salad, Frozen, 57
Fruit Salad Spectaculars, **48-63**
Fruit Salad Palermo, 61
Fruit Salad, Sunshine, 51
Fruit Sampler, 62
Fruit Tower, Party, 47
Garden Fresh Salads, **74-94**
Ginger Dressing, 49
Ginger Orange Dressing, 90
Ginger-Orange Mold, 40
Grapefruit Cup, Double, 55
Greek Country Salad, 11
Green Goddess Dressing, 19
Green Goddess Salad, 10
Green-and-Gold Salad, 80
Green Salad, Continental, 90
Green Salad with Grapes and Walnuts, 90
Guacamole Salad, 80
Guacamole Sauce, Peppy, 70
Guide to Buying Fresh Fruit, 52-53

H-L

Ham, Pineapple and Asparagus, Roquefort Mousse with, 11
Ham Salad with Mustard Dressing, Ziti and, 8
Herb Vinaigrette Dressing, 10
Herbed French Dressing, 21

Hollandaise, Mock, 19
Home-Style Salad Dressing, 20
Home-Style Tomato Dressing, 7
Honey Dressing, 50, 54
Honeydew Crescents, Frosted, 50
Honeydew Mold, Jeweled, 46
Horseradish Dressing, 32
How to Care For and Store Greens, 76
How to Make a Jellied Mold, 38
How to Pick Top Quality Greens, 81
How to Unmold A Jellied Salad, 34
Karrysalat, 10
Lemon Dressing, 60
Lobster, Cucumber-Rice Ring with Stuffed, 25
Lobster, Stuffed, 24
Lobster Salad in Artichoke Petal Cups, Shrimp and, 67
Lobster Salad Supreme, 72
Louis Dressing, 70
Louis Dressing Molds, 27
Luncheon Salad, 35

M-P

Macaroni and Mozzarella Salad, 87
Macaroni Salad, Seaside, 68
Mayonnaise, 19
Main Dish Salads, **6-21**
Melon Basket Salad, Buffet, 49
Melon Tray, Party, 51
Mexicali Salad Ring, 80
Molded Salad Riches, **22-47**
Mousse Ring, Buffet, 33
Mustard Dressing, 8, 80
Mustard, Savory, 19
Neptune's Tower, 72
Onion-Ring Salad Bowl, 86
Orange-Avocado Salad Bowl, 58
Orange-Pear Rosette, 61
Oriental Toss, 93
Papaya Coupe, 57
Parsley Chiffonade Salad, 89
Parsley Dressing, 44
Pear Rosette, Orange-, 61
Pear Salad, Honey, 62
Pears, Blue Cheese, 61
Pepper Baskets, Calico, 94
Perfect, The Chef's Salad, 9
Persimmon Salad, 54
Pineapple and Asparagus, Roquefort Mousse with Ham, 11
Pineapple Crown Salad, 58
Pineapple-Cucumber Salad, 61
Pineapple Royale, Frosted, 56
Plum Compote, 60
Portuguese Seafood Salad, 9
Potato "Chowder," Summer, 14
Potato Cones, 76
Potato Salad, Peruvian, 87
Potato Salad, Summer Garden, 75
Potato Salad a la Peloponnese, Main-Dish, 12
Potato-Salad Platter, Dilled, 75

R-S

Rainbow of Seafood Salads, **64-7**
Raspberry Chiffon Royale, 45

INDEX

Raspberry Cream Mold, 30
Rainbow-Fruit Mold, 30
Rice-Bowl Salad with Marinated Shrimps, Aloha, 66
Rice Ring with Stuffed Lobster, Cucumber-, 25
Rice Salad, Polynesian, 58
Rice Salad Layer, 25
Rijsttafel Salad Platter, 15
Rio-Rancho Supper Salad, 7
Roquefort Mousse with Ham, Pineapple and Asparagus, 11
Russian Dressing, 20
Salad Know-How, 12
Salad Greens, A Gallery of Popular, 78
Salad Nicoise, 65
Salata, 73
Salmon in Aspic, 29
Salmon Know-How, 73
Salmon Platter, Party, 23
Salmon Salad, Senegalese, 73
Salmon Supper Mold, 28
Sauce (*see also* Dressing), 8, 70
Sauerkraut Salad with Corned Beef, 9
Scallops, Marinated, 69
Scallop Salad, Cape Cod, 72
Seafood Salad, Portuguese, 9
Seaside Success, 71
Seaway Salad Bowl, 88

Shrimp and Lobster Salad in Artichoke Petal Cups, 67
Shrimp Aspic, Shimmering, 26
Shrimp-Cucumber Diadem, 37
Shrimp Cups, Tomato-, 83
Shrimps-Louis Dinner Salad, 12
Shrimp Salad, Bayou, 66
Shrimps Hawaiian, 65
Shrimps Marinated, 66
Slaw, Chinese, 91
Slaw, Farmer's, 92
Slaw, Triple Vegetable, 92
Spinach Salad, Tart, 89
Spinach-Tomato Salad Mimosa, 85
Spring Salad Bowl, 56
Squash Boats, Ruffled, 94
Strawberry Pink Dressing for Fruit Salads, 20
Stuffed Lobster, 24
Summer's Best Green Salad, 89
Sunburst Salad, 59
Sunday-Supper Salad, 87
Suyper Salad, 12
Swiss Cheese Salad, Egg and, 88

T-Z

Tangerine Salad Bowl, 58
Tangerine Sunshine Mold, 35
Thousand Island Dressing, 20
Tomato Dressing, Home Style, 7
Tomato Dressing, Piquant, 14
Tomato and Green Chili Sauce, 8
Tomato-Aspic Crown, 84
Tomato Bouquet Salad, 82
Tomato-Cucumber Cups, 82
Tomato Cups, Coleslaw-, 84
Tomato Cups Provencale, 84
Tomato Dressing, 69
Tomato Fan-Tans, 81
Tomato French Dressing, 21
Tomato-Kraut Cups, 85
Tomatoes Lutece, 81
Tomatoes, Relish, 81
Tomato Salad Mimosa, Spinach, 85
Tomato-Shrimp Cups, 83
Tomato Toppers, 38
Tuna Know-How, 71
Tuna Salad, Mediterranean, 7
Tuna-Salmon Mold, Glazed, 28
Tuna Supper Salad, 71
Veal Mousse, Red Cap, 39
Vegetable Bounty, Garden, 14
Vegetable Bowl, Green-and-Gold, 77
Vegetable Dressing, 90
Vegetable Relish, Fresh, 42
Waldorf Salad, Confetti, 62
Watermelon Bowl, Party, 50
Ziti and Ham Salad with Mustard Dressing, 8